WHAT'S HAPPENI

QUARRY BANK?

AN ALBUM OF
MEMORIES, PICTURES, & STORIES
BY
NED WILLIAMS

AND THE

MOUNT PLEASANT LOCAL HISTORY GROUP

Gladys Davies, John James, Bessie Cranton, Margaret Priest,
Marie Billingham, Bram and Vera Dunn, Ossie Biddle, Olive Allchurch,
John Robinson, Horace Dunn, Roy Smith, Mary Brookes, Jessie Yorke,
Charmayne Redding, Doris Peat, Pat Mattocks, Patrick & Slyvia Shaw,
Wesley Johnson, Fred Tipton, Gary & Sheila Marshall, Jane Geddes,
Doreen Cartwright, Joan Pearson and the late Arthur Pearson.

1999
URALIA PRESS

The Mount Pleasant Local History Group
was saddened by the death of Arthur Pearson
(1920-1999) in July. Arthur had made a huge
contribution to the work of the group by his
presence and by his first hand knowledge of
so many aspects of Quarry Bank history.
We appreciated his dedication to the group
and its work, plus his humour and encouragement.
Joan has allowed us to use the notes he had
prepared on a subject close to his heart - the
development of Quarry Bank from a political perspective.

What's Happened to Quarry Bank?
by Ned Williams and the Mount Pleasant Local History Group

ISBN 1 898528 06 3

First Published Autumn 1999

Uralia Press
23 Westland Road, Wolverhampton, WV3 9NZ

Credits: Photo processing by Jan Endean of Eardley Lewis, Temple St., Wolverhampton.
             and John James of the Local History Group.
             Screening by Galata Print, Llanfyllin, Powys.
             Maps drawn by Kiran Williams. Cover by Roger Crombleholme of Alphagraphix.
             Typesetting and layout by Uralia Graphics. Proof reading: Philip Barnard.
             Printed by Performance Print, Bromsgrove.

What's Happened To Quarry Bank?

CONTENTS

Having Fun in Quarry Bank!

Left: Mr. John Henry Stringer decorates his car and daughters for the Hospital Carnival in the 1920s. Harold Stringer on the left.
The Hospital carnivals carried on the tradition established by the Friendly Society Parades and Sunday School Processions of the days before the First World War, and were the predecessors of the modern galas.
(See pages 23 and 88)
(Mary Watson Collection)

Left: The Christ Church Young Wives Group celebrated their 25th Anniversary in 1973.
Activities included a hat-making competition. Left to right: Margaret Priest works on Bill Rennick, June Grove works on Vicar Irwin, Anne Homer works on Ray Grove, Maureen Genner works on Stan Reede and Jeanne Haywood works on Frank Lloyd.
(June Grove Collection)

Left: Waiting for something to happen in Quarry Bank: Martin and Ross Bevan and others congregate at the filling station that was built on the site of the Coronet, after meeting at the Sheffield Street community Centre.
(Sarah Vaughan Collection)

4

Introduction

Welcome to our latest book about Quarry Bank - a product of the work of the Mount Pleasant Local History Group.

We meet every Friday afternoon during term-time at Mount Pleasant Primary School in Quarry Bank to enjoy talking about the past and present of the local community. We operate as a class organised by the WEA - the Workers Educational Association, with the school acting as our host and provider of accommodation and refreshment. We have been meeting regularly since September 1997.

Our first publication was "110 Not Out!" - the story of Mount Pleasant School - which was published in September 1998 to mark the school's 110th anniversary. We quickly followed that with "Quarry Bank in Old Photographs" which was published at the end of October 1998. This venture was part of the Black Country sub-series of books produced by Sutton Publishing in their "Britain in old Photographs" series.

While compiling the book of old photographs we were aware that another book was growing out of our activities - a book that would be in a format that allowed some of the stories and factual information about Quarry Bank to be put in print. This is the book which sets out to fulfil that objective.

We have *not* tried to write the definitive and comprehensive history of Quarry Bank. What we have done is explore our own interests and put them together in some kind of order, creating something we have subtitled "An Album of Memories, Pictures and Stories". We hope that you will read this book in conjunction with "Quarry Bank in Old Photographs"[1] - and you will discover that they complement each other. If your favourite aspect of Quarry Bank's story seems to be left out of this book, you may find it is covered in the other, and vice versa.

This book is very much the work of individuals contributing to the over-all work of the group. Therefore I have tried to give credit to the work of identified individuals wherever possible. It is also true that everyone in the group adds what they can to the work of everyone else. Outside the group there are hundreds of people we have consulted and who have loaned us photographs, newspaper cuttings and items ranging from enamelled matchbox covers to silver medals. This makes the task of acknowledging everybody's contribution very difficult!

You will see that the title of the book poses a question. The book does not provide a final and conclusive answer to that question - but it does provide lots more food for thought! We certainly don't allow ourselves to become overwhelmed with doom and gloom by taking the line that Quarry Bank has "gone to the dogs"! I think we take the line that there has been change, and the present certainly does provide challenges in terms of maintaining the identity of Quarry Bank and preserving the obvious strong sense of community that it has enjoyed over the years.

The photographs and stories collected here show a Black Country town that was smaller than some of its neighbours, but a town that had quite a distinct character and was full of activity that helped build a sense of belonging - ranging from sporting activities, dramatic activities, carnivals, galas and horticultural shows, the work of local churches and political parties and so on...

The downside of the changes that have taken place within recent memory include the loss of many local industrial employers. This, and the massive expansion of housing in and around Quarry Bank, have made it much more of a "dormitory" community. Changes in retailing have meant that its once bustling High Street seems much quieter. Changes in the organisation in local government have made that government seem even more remote. The arrival of the Merry Hill Complex right on Quarry Bank's doorstep can seem to represent the welcome arrival of new jobs and easy access to a very bright and modern face of the Black Country, or it can be seen as something that overshadows Quarry Bank and creates traffic problems and a threat to the survival of local shops etc.

The strengths of Quarry Bank are things that are not necessarily found in other parts of the Black Country and should therefore be exploited positively. First of all Quarry Bank has not been deserted by the Quarry Bankers. This is a major asset to the community - there are still many people alive and well in Quarry Bank who have strong roots in the town - their names litter the pages of this book. Two other "assets" are the town's "size" and the survival of its special "geography".

Most Quarry Bankers have emerged from just three primary schools (four, if we include Withymoor as part of today's Quarry Bank) and in the past most Quarry Bankers emerged from the two Secondary Schools - one for boys, one for girls. Today, Thorn's Community School could be the common ground on which most Quarry Bankers have met and got to know one another. Larger towns never have the chance to establish common ground among young residents in this way.

Then there's the "geography". Despite residential expansion of the built environment of Quarry Bank, the town is still different to every other Black Country town. This is the result of having grown up as a town made up of small distinct communities - scattered isolated hamlets: Dunns Bank, Birch Coppice, Mount

---

[1] Referred to as "QBiOP" on later pages.

5

Pleasant, The Thorns, etc. Between these communities were tracks crossing open space that may have become pasture but was probably derelict waste that had once been mined for coal or fireclay. These communities, although isolated, grew in relation to the basic road structure of Quarry Bank - a cross with the junction of High Street and Thorns Road/Merry Hill at its centre.

The unique Quarry Bank experience is still easily enjoyed by walking away from this basic road pattern into what seems like a cul-de-sac. What seems like a dead-end, seldom turns out to be one. Instead it becomes a path or passage that takes you into a different "subsection" of Quarry Bank! Other parts of the Black Country have their towpaths and town-trails. Quarry Bank offers a labyrinth.

Explore this labyrinth and you will find a great deal of Quarry Bank's heritage survives, ranging from its elegant park, to good quality Victorian and Edwardian housing. It is still possible to walk "The Pipes" towards Cradley Heath, or go in search of farms out and beyond Caledonia. Quarry Bank still has traditional shops, friendly pubs, and splendid views from the top of the "bonk".

That brings me to one final matter. How should you pronounce "Quarry Bank"? As a "furriner", I am acutely aware that this can be a problem! In most places in this book we have stuck to the "standard" spelling. However, the local "Black Country" pronunciation of the vowel sound represented by the "a" in "Bank" is a delicate matter. I'll take the coward's way out, and leave it ter yo'.

Ned Williams
Autumn 1999

Below: The Mount Pleasant Local History Group.

Acknowledgements:
The Mount Pleasant Local History group currently consists of: Gladys Davies, John James, Bessie Cranton, Margaret Priest, Marie Billingham, Bram and Vera Dunn, Ossie Biddle, Olive Allchurch, John Robinson, Horace Dunn, Roy Smith, Mary Brookes, Jessie Yorke, Charmayne Redding, Doris Peat, Pat Mattocks, Patrick & Sylvia Shaw, Wesley Johnson, Fred Tipton, Gary & Sheila Marshall, Jane Geddes, Doreen Cartwright, Joan Pearson. (Arthur Pearson worked with us up until his death in July 1999.)

We acknowledge the help of others who have been part of the group on previous occasions, including Janice Mills, Frank Whiley, Jack Williams, Ivy Astley, Ron and Emma Hanglin, and many who have visited us once or twice and have passed on information.

Thanks also to: Eric Attwood, Lilian Attwood, D.Baker, Bill Bawden, Jack Beddall, Julie Bird, Gwen Chapman, Rev. Tom Chapman, Robert Chell, Charles Cooper, E. Cox, J. Davies, Roy Day, Jabe Edwards, Tom & Sybil Genner, Jack Genner, S. Greenaway, Eric Grove, June Grove, Jeanne Haywood, Mary Hill, Stan Hill, Brenda Holloway, Walter Hughes, Ivy Homer, Vicky Horton, Geoff Jones, Hilda & Joyce Mantle, Nancy Marchant, Janet Mason, Philip Millward, Phyllis Prescott, S. Raybould, Ken Rock, Pauline Rollason, Mary Rousell, Clifford Shaw, John Shaw, Judith Simpson, Eric Stanton, Alan Southall, Edgar Taylor, Minnie Taylor, John Thompson, Celia Thorneycroft, Ken Tipton, M. Watson, John & Margaret Watton, Frank Webb, Frank Whiley, Dave Whyley, Joy Woodhouse, Gemma Wright, Don Manley, Val Jones, Doris Webb, Shirley Winwood, Bert Grove, David Cox, Madge Richards & Madeleine, Sue Smith, Eileen Thompson, Gladys Hall, Clarice Squires, Joyce Parkes, Joe Jones, Brian Wooldridge, Cyril Cartwright, Keith & Tony Tomlinson and their wives, Olwen Homer, Peter Rhodes, Margaret Yates, Tommy Jennings, Janet Kings, Roger Timmins, Evelyn Beswick, Brenda Pearson and Elsie Payne, Peter Glews, Sarah Vaughan Plus everybody we have omitted!

Thanks to Gail Bedford for providing our "foundations", to the libraries at Stourbridge, Brierley Hill and Dudley Archives.

The last chapter would not have been possible without help from Joy and Paul Richardson, plus: Vic Raybould, Mary Fletcher, Stan Street, Ian Hampton, Margaret Davies, Carol Bannister, Ethel Bloomer, Mary Rousell, Betty Taylor, John Mason, Beryl Broome, Harry O'Malley, David Bennett, Roy Peacock, Margaret Webb, Mrs. A. Reynolds, Miss D. B. Cartwright, Bob Plant, Stan Robins, June Grove, Robert J. Clarke, Mrs. Joy Parkes, and others......

Chapter 1
Local Politics and the Development of Quarry Bank

Based on the work of Arthur Pearson

The earliest settlements at Quarry Bank were farms and farm-worker's houses, but some industrial development followed Dud Dudley's construction of the Cradley Forge on the River Stour in the early 17th. Century. The forge supplied wrought iron which could be supplied to local chainmakers and nailmakers. Local civic affairs were administered from the church vestry, and the courts of the Lord of the Manor, and the Quarry Bank area was the southernmost part of the Parish and Manor of Kingswinford.

The Manorial Courts were run by the Lord's Steward, who in turn appointed a 'Biddle' who summoned the court and collected fines imposed by it. A 'Reeve' was appointed to supervise agricultural matters, and a 'Forester' protected the Lord's timber rights. Early maps suggest there was a Foresters cottage in the Quarry Bank area. None of these officials provided what we would now regard as 'local government', and the small population was rather scattered. Small settlements grew into hamlets, but there was not much sense of these growing into a town. This is reflected by the fact that even today Quarry Bank can be broken down into quite separate parts.

Quarry Bank acquired 'parish' status in 1845 when the old Parish of Kingswinford was reorganised, and construction of Christ Church began close to the road that descended from the bank followed by the Amblecote Road down into the Stour Valley, and close to the point where that road crossed the route from Dudley to the Lye. Such roads were not surfaced, maintained, drained or lit. The move towards providing local government for the growing population was stimulated by the passing of the Local Government Act of 1867. This led to establishing a District Committee for Roads, and a Local Board of Health. Reverend Dixon, the Vicar of Christ Church, became the Board of Health's first chairman when it convened in 1867.

These early committees laid out the road pattern in central Quarry Bank on which the Victorian town began to grow. By 1868 they were asking the South Staffordshire Water Company to supply mains water to Quarry Bank, and investigating the provision of a post office. Twenty years later, in 1887, a report complained that Quarry Bank was still not systematically sewered, midden privies were foul and neglected, and that mains water only reached 20% of local houses. (The rest used springs and wells.) New powers were given to the County Councils at the end of the 1880s, and in the following decade "Urban Districts" were created in areas where it seemed likely that there would be enough revenue from "rates" to provide services at a local level. Quarry Bank became an Urban District in 1894.

The first councillors who took control of Quarry Bank Urban District were elected by a small male franchise. The Councillors, therefore were all men, and were Liberals or Conservatives. There was no challenge to this situation until the First World War. In 1916 J.C. Mason, a member of the Independent Labour Party, was appointed to the Local Food Committee, and the administration of War Pensions, although there was no local Labour Party operating in Quarry Bank until just after the War.

The local Labour Party transformed the politics of Quarry Bank following its formation in 1920. The party gained three seats in the 1922 elections.

After the election of 1925 an interesting situation arose when it came to electing the Chairman of the UDC. The council consisted of three Liberals, four Tories, four Labour and one 'ex-serviceman'. The Liberal vote was split, two voting in favour of a Tory Chairman, and one voting for a Labour. The previous Chairman had stood down to let the clerk run the meeting, but then returned to use a 'casting vote'. This caused a furore and was regarded as illegal, but several weeks elapsed in which the council was unable to resolve the issue and reconvene - all recorded in great detail in the County Express who urged the Quarry Bankers to find a compromise and "get on with it."

Labour took control in Quarry Bank in 1927 (7 Lab, 3 Tory, 2 Lib), and the first woman to be elected to the Council took her seat - Mrs. W.G. Cook, a local mid-wife, and Labour supporter.

Quarry Bank was never an affluent authority and the UDC was continually faced with financial problems. In 1934 it was "swallowed up" by the enlargement of Brierley Hill and therefore ceased to be a self-governing unit from that moment onwards. Quarry Bankers from then on elected two councillors from two wards: Thorns and Coppice. In 1934 all four seats were taken by Labour.

In 1937 one of the seats was lost to the Tories, but in the first post-war election, in 1946, all four seats were held by Labour once again. In 1952 the Council was reorganised and Quarry Bank was allocated three seats for each of its two wards. All six were then won by Labour, but in 1956 one of the Coppice Ward seats was won by the Tories. In the 1960s, the Tories also took one of the Thorns Ward seats for a time.

In 1966 Brierley Hill itself was swallowed up. It became part of the new County Borough of Dudley, thus moving from Staffordshire to a detached part of Worcestershire! This state of affairs only lasted eight years as the West Midlands County was created in the reorganisation of 1974. The 1974 changes also saw the

Local Politics and the Development of Quarry Bank

ward boundaries in Quarry Bank were re-drawn, partly reflecting the growing population in Withymoor. In the West Midlands County Council, Brierley Hill and Quarry Bank were represented by one seat, but that council was also short-lived and was abolished in the 1980s. Since then Quarry Bankers have 'enjoyed' single tier local government and simply return three councillors to Dudley MBC.

Despite the loss of identity that results from being administered by a large local government organisation, councillors are often still identified by their connections with a particular patch they have represented or in which they have their roots.

(Arthur Pearson acknowledged the help of the Libraries at Brierley Hill and Stourbridge, and the Dudley Archives at Coseley, when researching this topic, as well as help from Mrs. A. Heydon and Mrs. E. Payne (nee Homer).)

THE URBAN DISTRICT COUNCIL OF QUARRY BANK.
1926-27.

COUNCILLORS.
Elected April, 1925.

Mr. RALPH HOMER, 3, Dunn's Bank
(Chairman).

Mr. SAMUEL YARDLEY, 27, New Street
(Vice-Chairman).

Mr. JOHN HENRY STRINGER, Oak Villa, Oak Street.

Mr. HERBERT DUNN, Ashleigh, Thorns Road.

Mr. GEORGE COURT, 3, Level Woods.

Mr. JOHN FOXALL, 37, Merry Hill.

Mr. JOHN WILLIAM GENNER, 64, High Street.

Mr. SIMEON WOOD, 19, Dunn's Bank.

Mr. WILFRED SHAW, 69, Thorns Road.

Mr. CORNELIUS ALLPORT, 150, High Street.

Mr. SAMUEL JOSHUA BLOOMER, 3, Coppice Lane.

Mr. JAMES THOMAS WHILEY, 50, Mount Pleasant.

Left: Crowds make their way up the High Street to celebrate the election of Charlie Sitch in 1918. He was one of the four successful Labour Party MPs from the Black Country out of 58 that were returned nationally in a "khaki" election in which the Labour Party was standing for the first time in the form that we know it today.

Left: King George V's Coronation on 23rd June 1911 was celebrated with parades, feasts and firework displays all over the country. Quarry Bank UDC struggled to find the money to lay on much of a celebration but local benefactors came to the rescue and two days of events were organised. Here we see a Friendly Society group followed by what appear to be the Boys Brigade, passing down the High Street.

(Margaret Yates Colln.)

8

Chapter 2
Looking Back

In 1964 Don Manley was a teacher at the Quarry Bank Boys' Secondary School in Coppice Lane. One thing he did before he left Coppice Lane to go to Dudley Technical College, was to undertake a project with some fourth form boys which involved them interviewing eighty-year old Quarry Bankers to find out about life at the turn of the century. The interviewees, then aged about eighty, were only asked a narrow range of questions but the surviving documentation shows that quite a few well-remembered Quarry Bankers took part and their answers provide a tantalising glimpse of their memories of life at the turn of the century.

Looking back at memories of their home life at the turn of the century, interviewees thought that most homes were small and overcrowded, and were generally dingy. Black-leaded grates and podged rugs were a feature of everyone's home. People baked their own bread, kept their own pigs or fowl, and brewed their own beer.

Most of the people interviewed recalled school days in big classes, working on slates with slate pencils. Generally everyone felt that life had been "hard" and that living conditions and working conditions had been bad. People walked everywhere and leisure time was very limited. Treats, and escape from the daily grind, took the form of trips to Kinver or the Clent Hills, sometimes on foot, and sometimes by horse-drawn brake. A few examples of notes made of interviews are given below:

In 1964 the Quarry Bankers then in their eighties could remember the death of Queen Victoria (1901) and Boer War events like the Relief of Ladysmith. The latter was celebrated in Quarry Bank by putting out flags and children marching up and down the High Street. Controversy surrounded a question of whether the vicar had stopped someone ringing the church bells, but Rev. McNulty denied this and said that it had been a misunderstanding! Several interviews recalled mining operations in the New Street area that caused the chapel and some houses to collapse.

Don felt that he learnt a lot about the past in Quarry Bank from Ralph Homer, and indeed 79 year old Ralph was one of the Quarry Bankers interviewed. Ralph Homer was born in New Street, the son of a chain-maker. He left school at the age of twelve to become a chain-maker for Attwoods in Rose Hill, and later worked at The Judge - Ernest Stevens' holloware works at Cradley Heath. Thinking about his memories of life at the turn of the century, Ralph recalled some of the ways in which life was hard, the prevalence of drunkenness and the neglected state of people's homes. He remembered things improving in the first decade of the century and the talk of trams coming to Quarry Bank. (They never came!)

Mrs. Hough of 50 Dunns Bank was nearly 82 when interviewed. She had gone to Mount Pleasant School as a child and was taught by Mr.Hunt. Her father worked in an ironworks near The Delph but had "run away" to America for over thirty years. She did not see him again until after her mother's death. On leaving school she had gone into service as a maid for a family at Harts Hill, and only visited her own home at weekends. When asked about entertainment in the 1900s, she recalled going to the theatre in Cradley Heath.

Mrs. Price of 55 Amblecote Road was 78 when interviewed. Her father had worked in the pits at The Delph, and her mother was a brick moulder. She had started school at Mount Pleasant at the age of three and had left at thirteen to start work for E.J. & J. Pearson's brickworks. She worked there for sixty years, and her memories of the 1900s were working without shoes or socks, working long hours, and one particular night when a pit at The Delph collapsed.

Eva Shaw of 130 Amblecote Road was 88 in 1964. She was one of twelve children and her father was a wheelwright at Hill & Smith's. She had started work at the age of eleven - in service to a family at Wollaston. She worked for a month at a time with one day off at the end of each month, and worked "unlimited hours". Her general comment was that she preferred life in the 1900s to life in the 1960s!

Florence Batham of 3 King Street was 90 and had lived in Quarry Bank all her life. Her father had been a miner working in pits at Netherton, and she left school at 11 to work for Bloomers, making chains twelve hours day for 2/6d a week. She recalled the times when water had to be carried to people's homes from wells, and the days when Quarry Bank was a village surrounded by fields. She recalled making "pop" from dandelions and, like many others, remembered the fair coming annually to Oak Street. Legend told of a stabbing incident that had occurred at the Quarry bank Wake in the 1850s and some people called the fair "Stabman's Wake"!

Members of the Mount Pleasant Local History Group, meeting in the 1990s, often look back at the "old days" and consider how things have changed nationally and locally. Naturally we cannot go back as far as the people interviewed by Don Manley's students in 1964, but it is interesting to note that not much had changed by the inter-war years. Poverty and employment insecurity were still problems, sanitation and public health had improved but people's homes were still modest compared to present day expectations and people's memories of their schooling were still distinctly "Victorian". See the section devoted to individual memoirs appearing later in this book.

Points from the Parish Records for 1900

In the year 1900 about 160 children were baptised at the parish church. There were thirty six marriages, and about a quarter of the people who had to sign the register could only do so by making their "X". The majority described themselves as chainmakers, colliers or labourers. In 1900 111 people were buried in Quarry Bank - thirty three were children less than one year old, a further twenty were children under ten. The church itself went through various extensions and improvements in 1900, suffered a fire, and had to decide what to do about the fact that the church yard was becoming overcrowded. (In 1903 a new cemetery was opened alongside Victoria Road, was consecrated by Bishop Anson, and a tiny iron chapel was erected there.)

Above: The old face of Sheffield Street: old houses and chain-making shops awaiting demolition in the 1950s.
(Phil Millward)

Two photographs from Dawn Shaw's collection showing how the isolated communities of old Quarry Bank used to look.

Most cul-de-sacs set out from the High Street axis of Quarry Bank and became tracks by the time they reached the isolated areas of settlement. Belle Vue did the opposite. It set out from Coppice Lane by stopped well short of the High Street!

Many cottages in areas such as these were early 19th century and belonged to the first wave of urbanisation of the Quarry Bank area as nailers and chainmakers built their homes and workshops close to the supply of iron.

Chapter 3
The Changing Face of
Quarry Bank

The Pipes

Right: Laying the sewage pipe across the shallow valley of the Mousesweet Brook from Cradley Forge to Cradley Heath.

Right: "The Pipes" are laid and partly buried in an embankment. They are now covered in dense vegetation in an area partly traversed by tracks leading to the Saltwells Nature Reserve. Once they provided a meeting place for Quarry Bankers seeking some privacy out on the frontier of their town.

Quarry Bank is full of passages and entries that lead into areas of open ground, or link streets in unexpected ways. In recent years the open land has been built on, the roads and tracks joined, destroying the isolation of parts of Quarry Bank. This 1953 picture illustrates the way The White City, Belle View and Birch Coppice were isolated from the end of Sheffield Street.

11

One of the most significant schemes to reclaim the derelict open spaces of Quarry Bank - largely created by the effects of mining coal and fireclays - was launched after the First World War to provide Stevens Park for the people of Quarry Bank. Ernest Stevens gave land and money to enable this to happen. Here we see the park being opened on 16th July 1921.

The park drew inter-war housing development away from the Victorian streets close to the High Street and started to create a Quarry Bank "suburbia". The park itself became a focus for the fetes held in association with the Hospital Carnivals, and the more recent galas, and provided open space for football, bowls, tennis etc. In 1931 it became home to the Peace Memorial.

Here we see someone making for the park - from Park Road - in the 1960s.

(Mary Brookes Collection)

Geological instability has continued to be a problem in Quarry Bank right up to the present day. In the past, chapels have been defeated by subsidence and have disappeared. Now it is more likely to be housing that suffers.

Left: In January 1975 Grace Mountford watches the mechanical digger brought in to fill a hole that has suddenly appeared in her garden, in Wavell Road.

Chapter 4
Rural Quarry Bank

Margaret Priest

Introduction

Everyone old enough to remember an "old Quarry Bank" before the building of extensive modern housing can recall a community that was still partly rural. Indeed, rural Quarry Bank separated the town from its neighbours and helped preserve its identity. The spread of suburbia is not quite complete and one or two enclaves of the old rural aspect of Quarry Bank have survived. Margaret Priest decided to look into this and has assembled the following picture - augmented by some of the memories of the people concerned:

Freehold Farm

Many people may be surprised to hear that even in 1999 two farms are still in existence in the Amblecote Road area of Quarry Bank: Freehold Farm and Ravensitch Farm.

Freehold Farm House, which lies on the banks of the River Stour as it wends its way towards Stourbridge, looks much the same today as it did years ago when it was mainly a dairy farm run by William Chance. Nowadays sons Robert and Harry Chance live there. They can remember the Caledonia Housing Estate gradually replacing the little lanes, fields, scattered cottages, small-holdings, and mine workings - and the sewerage farm built in the 1940s and taking its name from Freehold Farm.

As a lad in the 1940s, Robert Chance sold milk, initially from the farm's own cows. The milk round grew as the number of houses in the area grew, and Robert delivered milk every day except Christmas Day. Robert knew every child's name and they looked forward to the daily pinta and the daily visit of his horse and cart. Children enjoyed taking a carrot or an apple to feed the horse. Over the years, several horses worked on the delivery - either named Tommy or Dolly, depending on their gender!

During the 1970s Robert won a "Milkman of the Year" competition run by Birmingham Dairies and the Sunday Mercury.

Nowadays Robert still delivers the milk, helped by brother Harry. There is no horse and cart unfortunately, but still the same excellent service, albeit by van. A couple of fields remain by the farmhouse, where two young horses graze, but these are pets, and the Chance Brothers couldn't bear to be without them.

Ravensitch Farm

Ravensitch Farm House, situated in an oasis of green amongst the housing estates, is just a few hundred yards away from Freehold Farm. Both farms retain their character despite the surrounding area changing so drastically. The Wright Family have farmed at Ravensitch for many years - going back to the time, in the early 1900s, when Samuel Thomas Wright came on the scene.

At the cottage in Woods Lane, then part of the farm, one of Mr. Wright's sons, Samuel Thomas, lived with his family while working for his father. It was there that the present farmer, also Samuel Thomas, was born. He was the second son; the name never being given to the first born son. This practice goes back several generations - perhaps to the 1700s - but nobody knows why. Perhaps the wives didn't like the name, and as the children were all known by their second name, it doesn't seem as if the children did either! The last three were referred to as Old Tom, Young Tom, and Young Tom's son - and it is Young Tom's son who is the present farmer.

In the early days, feeding cows was a much more labour intensive process. Before ready-mixed feed was in general use, the basic corns were bought from the corn merchants and mixed on the farm - adding roots such as mangolds and chaff. The chaff cutter was powered by a horse, attached by a pole to a gear which turned the chaff belts, working the cutters. The horse went round the gear in a circle, approximately 18' diameter.

Today there are just two cows: Fuzzbuzz, an Aberdeen Angus crossed with a Jersey, and her eldest daughter, Dinah - who is crossed with an Ayrshire, giving her horns. They are both very tame, having had much contact with Tom. Although the farm has shrunk to a couple of fields, it's a little piece of Quarry Bank that keeps alive memories of a time when there were fewer houses and more fields.

Mousehall

Mousehall Farm was in existence until the 1960s, but its history can be traced back hundreds of years. In "The Story of Pensnett Chase", D.R. Guttery tells us that Mousehall Farm was a Ranger's Lodge on the edge of the chase - recorded as early as 1665. Described as "a heathy, furzy, briary wilderness with coppices and woods", the banks of the Stour still retain remnants of how it must have once been.

Left: Fuzzbuzz and Dinah with Tom and Gemma Wright at Ravensitch Farm in 1999.
(Margaret Priest)

Mousehall Farm
Rugby pitches are now to be found on the site of the farm buildings.

Below: The Deeley Family Mousehall Farm.

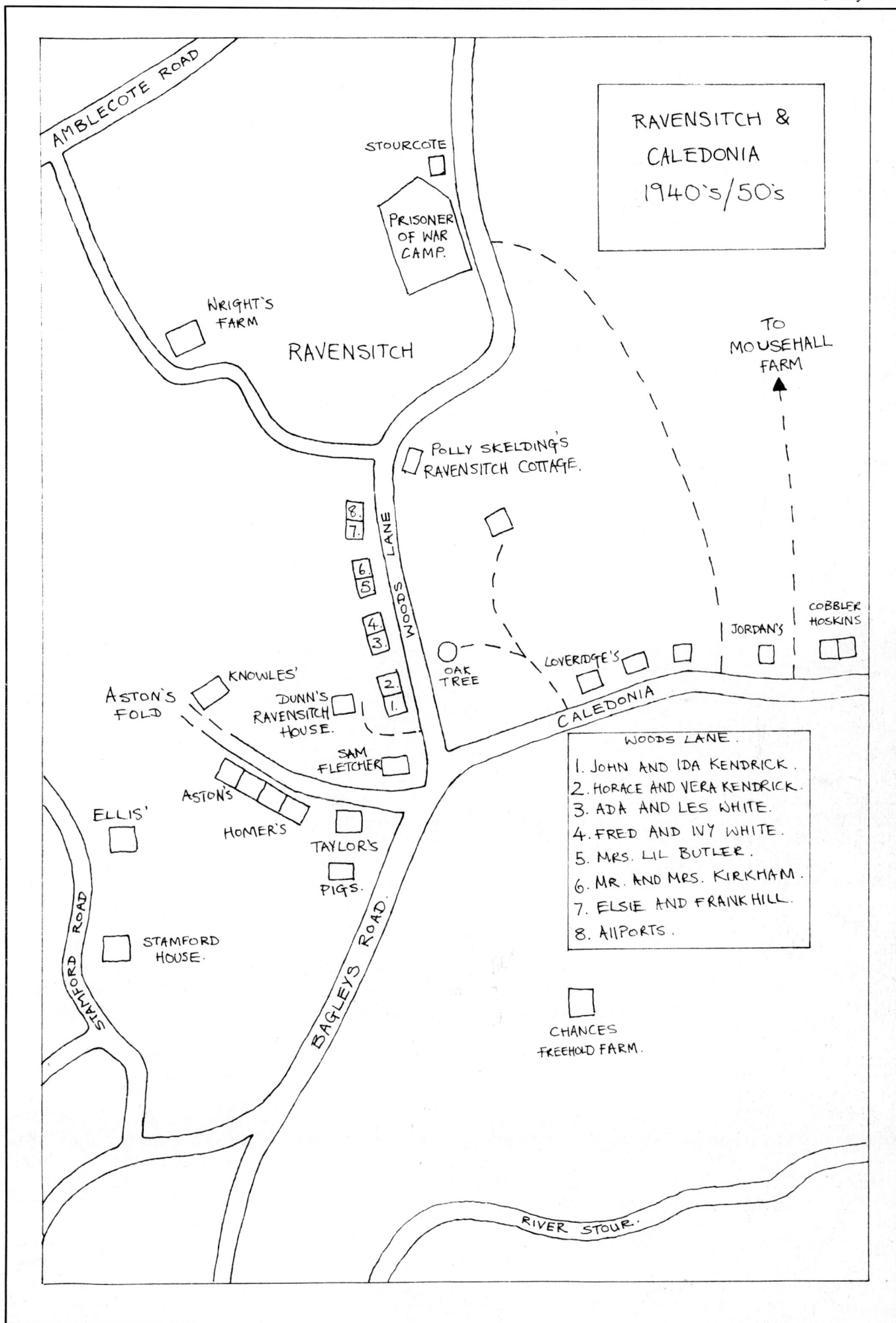

AMBLECOTE ROAD

STOURCOTE

RAVENSITCH & CALEDONIA 1940's/50's

PRISONER OF WAR CAMP.

WRIGHT'S FARM

RAVENSITCH

TO MOUSEHALL FARM

POLLY SKELDING'S RAVENSITCH COTTAGE.

8.
7.

WOODS LANE

6.
5.

4.
3.

COBBLER HOSKINS

JORDAN'S

KNOWLES'

2.
1.

OAK TREE

LOVERIDGE'S

ASTON'S FOLD

DUNN'S RAVENSITCH HOUSE.

CALEDONIA

SAM FLETCHER

ASTON'S

ELLIS'

HOMER'S

WOODS LANE.

1. JOHN AND IDA KENDRICK.
2. HORACE AND VERA KENDRICK.
3. ADA AND LES WHITE.
4. FRED AND IVY WHITE.
5. MRS. LIL BUTLER.
6. MR. AND MRS. KIRKHAM.
7. ELSIE AND FRANK HILL.
8. ALLPORTS.

TAYLOR'S

PIGS.

STAMFORD ROAD

STAMFORD HOUSE.

BAGLEYS ROAD

CHANCES FREEHOLD FARM.

RIVER STOUR.

Mousehall was probably one of the first houses to be built on the Chase, and the post of "ranger" was likely to have been "bestowed as a reward for favours done to, or anticipated by, the patron." The first ranger - going back to 1665 - was John Carey, who wrote the name of his house as "Mousall". The Carey Family lived there until the end of the eighteenth century.

It was Dud Dudley who was instrumental in changing much of the Chase from a "landlord's playground into one of the world's busiest workshops". The Industrial Revolution changed the land and its people forever. Coal, iron and steel, and clay became invaluable commodities. The clay mined from the Amblecote Bank was dark blue clay special to this part of the Stour Valley. It baked into a pale gold, and there was a clay which baked almost white which was used for making pipes.

In 1786 the land was allotted to new owners and Mousehall became part of Quarry Bank The last owner for whom it was still a farm was Winifred Hannah Plant Deeley, one of seven daughters, none of whom married. Stan Yardley inherited the farm - he had managed it for her in latter years. In 1968 the farm and land were compulsorily purchased by the council to make way for the new Thorns school. The site of the Rugby pitch is where the house once stood. So, should you chance to walk down Mousehall Farm Road, reflect on the history that has helped shape Quarry Bank!

Caledonia - recalled by Gemma and Tom Wright

Ravensitch Farm House is semi-detached, and when my Grandparents came to live here, almost a hundred years ago, they were given the choice of which house to have. They decided on the one nearest the cowsheds. The Trevis Family lived next door with their children; Arthur, Adam, Felix, Alfred, Alice, Priscilla and Maud. One day, Priscilla and her fiancee were doing a spot of courting in the parlour when they were rudely interrupted by a cow pushing her head through the window! The Trevises complained and a fence was erected to prevent any more embarrassments. After their parents had died and the girls had married, Arthur, Alf and Felix stayed on. Adam was married to Kate who used to come and do a spot of housekeeping, and later Maud, who lived in the cottage at the top of our drive in Amblecote Road, did the washing. It was Alfred who stayed at home to look after his brothers.

I remember Polly Skelding, a real character with a wicked sense of humour. She lived in Ravensitch Cottage on Woods Lane - not far below where the shops are now. Originally it had been her parents' home. The huge Japonica tree by the back door which had massive flowers twice a year had been grafted on apple stock by her mother, I was told. Most of her garden was down to soft fruit, particularly raspberries, which she sold.

Until the POW camp was built in 1943 her water was drawn from a well. She was talking to me one day and mentioned that Richie did her washing! I was flabbergasted and lost no time in telling my husband, Tom. He duly informed me that Polly was referring to white-washing her kitchen and outbuilding walls!! Richie was the local handyman/decorator. I also recall that Polly had a boisterous dog - Rover. The only admonition I ever heard her make was, "Down, Rover" - of which he took not the slightest notice.

When my brother Vince and I were little boys, we both had black hair, and without fail were coerced into bringing in the New Year for Polly Skelding. "Pipe it up, lads," she would order, as we presented the requisite piece of coal, and was not satisfied until we'd been through all the house. We were then rewarded with a mince pie. One year we were sent to Sarah Smith's to do the honours. She was very upset and irate, much to Polly's amusement when we returned home.

Another memorable person was Teddy Hoskins, a bachelor who lived with his mother along Caledonia, before you reached the Staffordshire House Pub. He was a shoemaker and repairer, and worked in a shed at the back of his cottage. He delivered repaired shoes in a little black cloth bag, on foot, and at great speed. On Sundays in the summer he often cycled into the country, chiefly around Martley, near Great Witley, and I remember that he always gas-tarred the side of his house against the prevailing south west wind.

The Prisoner of War Camp was built on our 'Swing Field' in 1943 - so called because there was a swing fixed to the oak tree. When it was being built my mother-in-law, Mrs. Lizzie Wright, was talking to the sergeant in charge and said she didn't want rubbish to be thrown over onto the rest of the field. "Oh no," he replied. "You'll find they're a tidy lot."
"There's no such thing as a tidy lot - there's always some!" she retorted.

In the middle of what is now Astons Close, lived Sam Fletcher in Kimberley Cottage. His haulage business was started from there. Mrs. Fletcher used to have her milk delivered by one of the Wright lads twice daily. She'd put her thumb in the basin and if wasn't still warm she would refuse it as 'not fresh'.

At no. 7 Astons Fold, later moving to no. 8, lived Mr. Homer. His son, Arthur, still lived there until recently. He made frost cogs for horses shoes. And at no. 9 there was Mr. Ashton, a cripple, father of Lydia who was Kath Wright's mother. (No relation to us.) Dick Aston also had a house in Aston's Fold. Another Aston, Bob, lived in a cottage just a stone's throw away. Some of these cottages are still in existence, tucked away opposite Caledonia (Road).

The Dunns lived at Ravensitch House, in between our farm and Astons Fold, as I recall. Just over the Quarry Bank border, off Stamford Road, was Stamford House, originally inhabited by a bailiff for the Enville Estate.

Caledonia - recalled by Sylvia Shaw

My abiding memory of Caledonia is of the prisoner-of-war camp; although known locally as "the German prisoner of war camp", in fact it also contained Italians. It would be about 1945, when I was six: when going on Sunday walks with my older sisters we used to pass the perimeter fence and watch them digging in their allotment, or washing themselves under the outside tap, dressed only in their trousers. I thought they looked rather sad.

One old lady I knew who felt sorry for them would invite them for Sunday lunch. To repay her kindness they dug her garden. I believe this also applied to other local residents.

Another memory is of picking catkins and blackberries down the lanes, and walking through the fields on warm sunny days seeing horses and cattle in the shade of the trees.

Caledonia - recalled by Arthur Pearson

It seemed to me that the houses down Woods Lane and the cottages spread about Caledonia were a little hamlet hardly belonging to Quarry Bank. Well known to be solid Labour, come election time transport was always made available to the polling station at Mount Pleasant School.

When I was about twelve I had to deliver meat by push bike from a butchers in the High Street down to the Caledonia. The Jeavons Family would have a brisket of beef weighing six or seven pounds for 4d! And Mrs. Jeavons, a lovely lady, would give me apples and pears for my trouble.

Right: Freehold Farm today with the two resident horses. This is the view looking across the Stour valley.
(Margaret Priest)

Right: The Caledonia open-cast in 1961, where Grosvenor Way and Winding Hill are now located.
(Margaret Priest)

17

Caledonia - recalled by Val Jones

My recollections of childhood go back to when I was being brought up in one of the few houses in Woods Lane. My home life centred on the gravelly lane - a good mile or more from Quarry Bank, even across the fields.

We lived in one of the eight "new" houses, towards the bottom of the hill where Woods Lane joins Caledonia (Road) and Bagleys Road. In those days, almost sixty years ago, Ravensitch and Astons Fold was our playground, and Caledonia was an expanse of fields and mine-workings, cottages and farms.

The 'village' was school, church and shops, but 'home life' was playing in the fields. On the opposite side of our road was a hedge of snowberry bushes, and we children made gaps in the hedge to the field and to the large old oak which was our meeting place, and the focal point of our many games: tick, hide-and-seek, etc., and the patch of ground near the tree was also the site of many bonfires.

During the winter the single street lamp took over: no passing cars to worry about even when playing 'kick the can'. As the lamp was at the top of the hill outside Polly Skelding's house, and opposite Wright's Farm, the can invariably rolled down to the bottom giving players a longer time to hide.

One day, playing bat and ball with my friends, I gave the ball a mighty swipe which unfortunately sent it straight through Polly's window. The children scattered - but there was trouble to pay! They all vowed not to tell who the culprit was, but somebody let the cat out of the bag and told my Mom and Dad who were very angry, mostly because I had not owned up. My Dad subsequently replaced the window, but I had to go and apologise to Polly. This in itself was the worst punishment I could have received - Polly seemed to us children to be a very fierce old lady, and there was always a black cat sitting in her window. 'Was she a witch?' we wondered.

Scrumping was another favourite occupation. Oh what delicious terror to climb into the orchard at Stamford House just down the lane, and then out again with the precious booty but without being caught. On one such sortie, coming home with jumpers stuffed full of apples and pears, we had to cross the brook which marked the Quarry Bank border. (Sadly, this brook has long since disappeared.) Rushing to keep up with the others, I missed the far bank, and fell in the water, and lost all my precious cargo. Then, soaking and bedraggled, I had to go home and get out of it as best I could!

The years have flown by and much has changed but our house is still there - although the snowberries, the fields, and our oak tree have been replaced by houses.

Below: Looking down into the Stour Valley from Caledonia in 1998. This landscape will change again if the sewage treatment works closes, affecting the wedge of open land stretching from here to Freehold Farm.

Chapter 5
Quarry Bank at Work

Introduction

At a time when Quarry Bank started to grow into a small town, most of the working population were engaged in nail making and chain making. Others worked in the coal and fireclay pits, and a few walked to neighbouring towns like Cradley Heath, Netherton, the Lye and Brierley Hill to work in their metal industries. As the town grew the workforce widened to include a greater variety tradesmen and craftsmen, and some of the industry became more factory based. The holloware industry became a large employer in the south western corner of the Black Country and many people worked at 'The Judge' at Cradley Heath and 'The Jury' in The Thorns. Other important local firms were Brettell & Shaw, Tubular Holloware, Bird-Stevens, B. H. Castings, Hanke's, Warwick's etc...

This chapter casts a glance at the world of work - starting with Joan Pearson's enquiry into the business of just how much have Quarry Bankers had to go quite far afield in search of work, followed by an attempt to give a personal view of the history of The Jury. Margaret Priest worked with 92 year old John Robinson to provide this story, and we turn to another 92 year old - Bert Grove - to provide some of his first hand experience of working at The Jury. We take a passing look at a few other aspects of the Quarry Bank world of work like Malin's and the daily exodus to the BSR.

A few thoughts on

Why People Left Quarry Bank to Seek Work

By Joan Pearson

Up until the First World War the work that was available locally was dominated by chain-making, holloware manufacture, local mining of coal and fireclay, small engineering and commerce (shops etc). However, during the First World War women were working as far afield as Birmingham in munitions factories.

Many people had been forced to work locally and had experienced poor conditions and were therefore not content to see their children do the same. They encouraged their offspring to look for jobs further afield, hoping to improve their living standards and broadening their outlook.

This was made easier with the introduction of train and bus services that linked Quarry Bank with the outside world. Some people simply "got on their bikes". My own father did just this, and my late husband told me that at the age of sixteen he cycled to Longbridge - to the Austin Motor Company - for a job interview. For many years a train service was provided to take workers from the Black Country to the Austin, and also local coach proprietors ran regular services. (Bert Homer from Quarry bank, and Shuker's of Halesowen picked up men from the Queens Head in Quarry Bank.) Some people made their way to Brierley Hill and caught the train to Kidderminster to work in the carpet trade.

Although the average working day was 7am to 5pm. with one hour dinner break plus Saturday 7am to 12.30.pm, the much improved working conditions and pay compensated for the extra travelling time. The lengthened working day soon became a way of life - I can vouch for this from experience. At the age of fifteen I travelled to Birmingham city centre for training as a comptometer operator, and remained in employment with city companies until I became a wife and mother. The local companies had no scope for comptometer operators. Now, of course, it is very different - the comptometer has been superseded by the calculator and the computer, and all businesses now use them.

Another factor in the movement of labour has been the increase in population. The local industries did not expand correspondingly, and nowadays the distance from home to work is even greater for some people.

In 1981 Quarry Bank and Cradley had a relatively low proportion of the employed workforce engaged in the Service Sector activities:
50.4% compared with 57.22% on average in the Borough
39.62% worked outside the Borough - very close to the average of 39.39%
23% worked in professional and managerial/technical occupations compared with a Borough average of 32%

Then there was a marked change. There was a huge increase in those employed in managerial and skilled non-manual occupations at the expense of manual working, even though the small number of unskilled workers had doubled in size. This could be a result, in part, of the opening of the Merry Hill Centre. A higher number travel to work by car - with other forms of transport decreasing. Compared with 1981 there has been an increase in the number of people working both at home and outside the Borough. Generally, manufacturing industry has contracted while the Service Sector has been considerably enlarged. There has also been a change in the hours people work.

(Joan acknowledges help from Brierley Hill Library in finding some statistics.)

Left: Mary Brookes from Quarry Bank is packing record decks at the BSR while some Japanese visitors are shown round. The BSR factory at Amblecote was the kind of employer that recruited in the Quarry Bank area in the 1960s.
(Mary Brookes Collection)

Left: Young workers at the Jury - John Stevens holloware factory at in Thorns Road.

Fifty Years Each in the Brick Yard!

Many Quarry Bankers worked in the fireclay pits and brickyards that stretched from the Delph across Withymoor towards Amblecote. These industries were associated with hard manual work, and surprisingly they were also associated with long-employment.

On the left are Richard and Elizabeth Cartwright - both proudly wearing the medals given to them by the Institute of Clayworkers for fifty years service - working for E. J. & J. Pearson Ltd. It must be unusual for a man and wife to clock up a century of working in the same business, but they had both worked for Pearsons all their lives. They both continued working beyond the 50 years and Elizabeth was most indignant about eventually being moved to lighter duties. They lived in Quarry Bank High Street and were active members of the congregation at Christ Church. They both lived until the age of 86.

(Photo and information from Marie Billingham)

20

The Jury

Edward Stevens and his wife came to live at the top of Thorns Road in Quarry Bank as a young married couple, having previously lived in The Lye. There were four children to the marriage: sons William, John and Ernest, and a daughter named Lucy. As a child, along with his siblings, John attended Mount Pleasant Wesleyan Church, although in later years he didn't belong to any particular church.

Having worked his apprenticeship to the bucket trade at Lye, John set up in business as a bucket manufacturer in Brick Kiln Street. In those days virtually the whole of production was carried out by hand. Unfortunately the premises were considerably impaired by subsidence and in the interests of efficiency new premises became necessary.

John had married Martha Elizabeth Weston, daughter of Samuel Weston of Brick Kiln Street. Home was what we now know as Coppice Close. Latterly they came to live in the "Cot" next to the works in Thorns Road, which had been opened in the early 1900s.

John Stevens' friend, Alfred Thomas Robinson, was to play a central part in building production at Thorns Road. He worked for the Peerless Bedstead Company in Old Hill, and when that firm went bust he went to see John Stevens. John was delighted…. "We'll have a go Alf. I've got some land but not a lot of money." And that was the birth of what became "The Jury".

There were out-houses at Coppice Close where Alf made patterns and tools. Meanwhile, John built the workshops and cupola on a piece of his land in Thorns. He owned land on both sides of the Thorns, giving some in trust for a school which eventually became Thorns Primary - many years later.

The new works were called John Stevens Bedstead Works, producing brass and iron bedsteads. Ann Rebecca, Alfred's wife, worked in the factory dipping the iron bedsteads in enamel. Most of the workers came from Dudley, probably having worked previously for the Peerless. As there was no direct tram line, the workforce generally walked to and from work.

Progress could not be taken for granted. At one stage twenty four year old Bert Stevens returned from America to find John Stevens, his uncle, in the depths of despair. A terrible storm had destroyed most of Jury Holloware, and John said he could not start all over again. Bert gave his uncle the support and encouragement he needed and together they rebuilt the business - much to the delight of the local population.

At one stage the business grew so rapidly that many extensions were made and the factory became one of the largest holloware works in the Midlands. In 1920 a branch was opened in Engine Lane, Lye, and at the time of his death over 1000 workers were in John's employ. They were known locally as 'John's angels'.

As the business expanded it became a pioneer for the holloware trade and it was Alfred who made the plaster of Paris patterns for the pie dishes, a new venture based on products made in Germany. And so The Jury - the trade name of John Stevens' firm - became major producers of kettles, and saucepans, with steel replacing cast iron.

Alfred eventually left the company to work for Oakleys Bedsteads but he and John remained firm friends. When Alf's son John was 14, in 1922, his father felt there could be no better employment than working for The Jury. Arriving on his first day at 8 o'clock in the morning young John was set to work in the packing department - nothing unusual you might think, but the boss worked alongside him for the whole of the first week! He was later transferred to work under Major Billingham making mounted forgings - bales for buckets and liners for bins. At 18 John progressed to being an enamel fuser in the furnaces, working on water bottles for the armed forces.

John Stevens owned other firms including the aluminium holloware works at the Lye, and the Hurst Firebrick Works at Woodside, formerly owned by Mobberley & Perry Ltd. At one time he farmed Round Hill Farm at Kinver, and owned farms at Albrighton and Deansford in Kidderminster. Work was his life and his main love. He rarely took time off. He was often up at five, and was sometimes seen going to the works during the night for an impromptu visit in his high boots and his long black overcoat covering his nightshirt! The story goes round that when the furnace foreman saw the light go on in the Cot, they sent a message round the works by tapping the pipes. Today he would be described as a workaholic, but for all that he was loved, almost idolised, by the workforce.

John was an approachable man, of great integrity, exceptional business ability, extremely generous, kind and well read. He held Quarry Bank in deep affection and subscribed to religious and social causes, preferring his name not to be mentioned. Politically he supported the Liberals, until in his later years he became a Tory.

Just six weeks before his death at the age of 78, the company turned public, becoming Jury Holloware (Stevens) Ltd.

Quarry Bank mourned the passing of John Stevens. At his funeral Thorns Road was lined with over a thousand workpeople and residents. Forty cars were needed to convey the mourners to Perry Barr for the cremation. John Stevens' ashes were scattered on the Clent Hills near to the Four Stones by his nephew Ernest, as was his wish.

Like his brother John, Ernest also set up a quality holloware manufacturing business - The Judge, but it was sometimes said that 'Ernest made for the classes while John made for the masses.'

Bert Grove's memoirs

I'm a real Quarry Bank "mon", born and bred in Z Street - born on 18th June 1907. My father, and his father, were also called Herbert Grove. I can remember Grandad Grove sitting on a low wall at the end of Sheffield Street, but Dad had gone to Scotland in search of work and then came back to Quarry Bank to be a furnace bricklayer for John Stevens. We moved from Z Street to 11a Thorns Road - our home was in a terrace of houses quite close to John Stevens' works.

As the works grew, my father would build new furnaces and undertook the maintenance of the works, becoming a sort of foreman or maintenance engineer for John Stevens. Job descriptions weren't too important, you simply worked "Down at John's" and worked hard doing whatever needed to be done. A little community grew up in Thorns Road whose lives revolved around the works. Our neighbours were the MacDonalds - and Mr. MacDonald had come down from Scotland to do the pipework, Carl Silk did the fitting and became a sort of Works Engineer. And then there were the Oakleys who helped John Stevens make bedsteads up at Mount Pleasant. John Stevens himself was always hard at work - wearing an apron just like everybody else - and if necessary he would make buckets just like his men. It was a real family place where everyone was kept busy - there was never a dull moment.

Once we had moved to Thorns Road, I had quite a long walk each day to school at Quarry Bank. I recall that there were two teachers who were brothers, Tom and Jim Butler, who also had a sweet-making business the other side of Cradley Heath. And I remember Simeon Wood - "Mr. Wood who came out of the wood" - as his family's home was in Dunns Bank. He was a real Quarry Bank man who did what he could for the place. But it is now too long ago to remember the names of the other teachers.

While at school I worked for Price's delivering their bread to customers in the Coppy (Birch Coppice), and I had a lot to do with my maternal grandparents in Cradley Heath. Grandad Howe worked for a famous Cradley Heath chain-making firm - going to work early in the morning to cut the rod into lengths, then having his breakfast before making the chain. Grandma Howell made chain at home in the yard, along with another woman, and many a time after school, I would make for Corngreaves Road, Cradley Heath to blow the bellows for Grandma for a penny a week.

When I left school I went to work for John Stevens where it was intended that I would work under my father and would learn bricklaying. But I was later made a boilerman, because, as I have said, everyone at John's mixed in and did whatever job came up and worked whatever hours were required. We didn't get paid much but we seemed to be happy, and everyone just accepted that we should work there. My sister Cissie also worked for John Stevens, making brushes and brooms, until she married a railwayman called Bert Nash, and they went to a council house close to Stourbridge engine shed.

Although I accepted a life where "pennies" were going to be around more than "pounds", I had always had the idea that "wherever there was a penny to be won, I had to win it", and I therefore changed jobs according to whatever I could find to do. I worked for various bucket-making firms in The Lye, but then I came back to John Stevens to drive the firm's steam lorry. I had always had an interest in such things and had even driven the steam engines for the showmen now and again. I remember the days when the Wake used to open on ground near New Street - before it went to the patch of ground off Oak Street, and I can remember when Pat Collins opened Lye Wake by the Cross.

John Stevens' steam lorry was a "Yorkshire Commercial", and the only other one like it in the area was run by the Midland Electric Company. John's lorry was painted dark red and part of my job was to keep it clean. I had to drive it to Shrawley on the far side of Stourport to fetch timber, or had to load it with crates that had to be taken round to Lye railway station. Later I drove a petrol lorry. I was still only a lad while doing all these things, but later worked for Midland Red, and for the railway.

While working for Midland Red I was based at Bearwood, and had to cycle between there and Quarry Bank twice each day - up and down hills. No wonder there never seemed much time for anything else except work. Even on Sunday mornings we had to be up promptly, and we had to fill in a card to record our attendance at Mount Pleasant Wesleyan Chapel - my parents were very strong church people.

Eventually I married Gladys May, a Wordsley girl. We married at Quarry Bank Church, but we went to live in Enville Road, Stourbridge and I returned to Midland Red. From then on I had less to do with Quarry Bank, but my parents continued to live in Thorns Road, and my father worked for John Stevens until he died.

Tubular Holloware

In 1916 John Henry Stringer (see page 88) joined forces with Ernest Billingham and George Cornforth to create the Tubular Holloware Company. They rented an old malt house for 5/- a week from G.J. Billingham - the building being next door to Mr.Stringer's house in Oak Street * - and employed four men to work an evening shift.

A decade later the firm employed 130 people and had expanded the premises considerably into the orchard that had surrounded the malt house. The firm seems to have been a very happy enterprise and J .H. Stringer soon had cricket and bowling teams organised and encouraged employees to participate in the annual hospital carnival. He also organised charabanc trips to the seaside for employees and their families.

The company exhibited its enamel ware each year at local 'Industry Fairs' and continued to prosper and expand even as Mr. Stringer's health failed - leading to his death in 1930. The firm survived until 1963.

Above right: Mr. Cornforth of Tubular Holloware with his wife, and on the left: Jack Brookes, who sometimes drove them about.
(Mary Brookes' Collection)

Right: The Tubular Holloware stand at the British Industries Fair at Castle Bromwich in 1929.
(Peter Rhodes Collection)

Right: The Tubular Holloware stand five years later has grown slightly larger.
(Peter Rhodes Collection)

Opposite page: Bert Grove, and his driver pause with their Midland Red bus at Old Hill.

* A picture of the Stringer Family at their home in Oak Street is to be found on page 89.

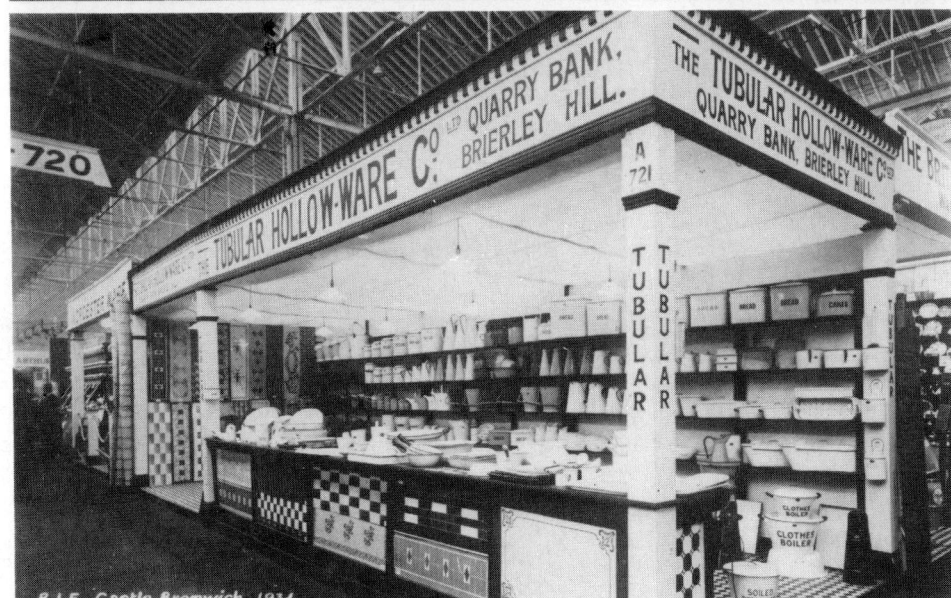

Local Builders:

Two building firms seem to have become well-known in Quarry Bank - one was Arthur Webb and Sons in Sun Street, the other was Cox's in Park Road.

Arthur Webb & Sons.

Arthur Webb was born in Ivy Cottage in Upper High Street, Quarry Bank, and as he grew up he trained as a carpenter - a trade in which he became very skilled. He set up his own carpentry workshop at the back of Ivy Cottage in 1887, and the business grew from there.

Arthur married Clara Maria Hazlehurst from another old Quarry Bank family and she was very supportive of her husband's work. She helped with the accounts and helped make decisions. Once Arthur had worked out that he could build some houses that could be sold for £195 each. His wife suggested that they be sold at £200 each - to be sure of making a profit! Typical of Arthur's work were the first fifteen houses in Victoria Road.

The Webbs had two sons Mervyn and Frank. Frank was born on 22nd August 1902. In 1998 Frank recalled:
"I went to Mount Pleasant School, which was a wonderful school, and then to Stourbridge Grammar School which entailed a three mile walk each way. All that was good training for what came next: I spent three years training with William Sapcote & Sons in Birmingham, and also attended night classes at Birmingham School of Art. I left Quarry Bank each morning at seven and was seldom home before ten at night, but I gained a good education and training to go into the building industry.

At Sapcotes I gained valuable experience in working with concrete, and learned much from the masons, painters, woodworking machinists and plumbers. I learnt everything except plastering and electrical work - and reckon I got ten years training in three! Whatever job I was given at Sapcotes, I had to find a way of doing it - I learnt never to say " I can't" or "I won't", and this stood me in good stead in later life. For example - I took on one or two jobs which I did not really know how to do - such as the demolition of the Rufford Works in Stourbridge, where I regret that I destroyed two beam engines that would have been valuable today.

My training gave me the confidence to take over my father's business in 1922 when I was twenty. He said, "O.K. - if you think you can do it better than me, you take charge." He was then sixty, so he was able to retire. He would come and look round and kept an eye on what I was doing, but he never interfered. As he was so gifted with his hands, he made a beautiful hand cart and kept himself busy.

The firm was always busy and we had very dedicated staff. I remember that once we had to recondition five schools for Staffordshire Education Authority in five weeks. I didn't know how we would get through it all, but the foreman painter re-assured me, and by that evening he had washed down five ceilings."

Frank's work played a part in the story of many local industries and enterprises. For example, he put in the foundations at Hingleys where many of the great liners' anchors were forged, and he became an expert on building annealing furnaces and brick-making kilns. (Frank became very keen on "domes" - which he puts down to having built so many kilns.) He also rebuilt the Jury Holloware works with concrete floors - replacing the original brick floors that John Stevens had laid over the contours of the ground as the works expanded.

Frank Webb also built many council houses in the area. The first that he built were in the Bluebell Wood, Saltwells, and he took considerable trouble to retain and preserve existing trees - only to see the first tenants chop them down for firewood. When Quarry Bank UDC was swallowed up by Brierley Hill, he built some houses in Thorns Road, followed by the Dunns Bank housing Scheme.

Frank also built houses in the 1930s on the opposite side of Upper High Street to the cottage in which he had been born. He lived in "Hillcroft" himself until moving to Stourbridge at the end of the War.

Frank Webb retired when he was eighty, but by the 1980s the firm had become a property firm rather than builders. After a long and busy working life Frank had the satisfaction of knowing that he and his father had built a great deal of the buildings to be seen in the area.

The Cox Family - Local Builders

Percy Cox (1889 - 1953) was a successful brick-layer who set up his own business in 1910 to seek contracts from local councils who were moving into house-building. One of his first contracts was for Dudley Council on the Holly Hall Estate. The First World War put a stop to this kind of work and Percy Cox diversified into furnace building etc. However, by the 1920s council house building had been resumed with a vengeance, and by the 1930s Percy Cox was building private houses on his own account over a wide area.

In 1929 Percy was joined by his elder son Bill Cox, and five years later by his younger son, Jack Cox. The Coxes' offices and headquarters in Park Road became a familiar part of the Quarry Bank landscape and the Coxes became part of the Quarry Bank "social scene". Jack Cox liked keeping pigs on the ground behind the offices, and reared pigs for supply to Marsh & Baxters in Brierley Hill. The land behind the offices was part of Dunn's Farm and when this land was no longer farmed the firm bought it and eventually built houses on it.

The roads around Park Road contain plenty of examples of Coxs' building work, even some cast stop-cock covers still bear their name! One building in Park Road deserves a special mention. Mr Oliver, the butcher, married and wished to move into a new house and shop on a site in Park Road. The premises were built in a record time of three weeks and can still be seen in use today.

After achieving so much from their base in Quarry Bank during the 1930s, the firm almost ceased to exist as a result of the Second World War. Jack Cox served in the Royal Engineers, and Bill Cox joined contractors working on aerodrome construction and maintenance.

After the War Bill started a small plant-hire firm in Shirley, but Jack eventually returned to the building business and found work locally. After Percy Cox's death in 1953, Bill's plant hire business rejoined the family building business in Quarry Bank.

Right: George Billingham and Percy Cox.

Below: Cox's premises in Park Road. Houses are now occupying this location.

(Both pictures: David Cox)

New undertakings, take-overs and mergers by 1968 produced a new group of companies trading as Cox - Leasows Ltd. with Jack Cox as the MD of the building companies and Bill Cox as MD of the plant hire business. In the 1980s the group moved to premises just outside Stourbridge.

Delivering Babies

Jessie Gullick came to Quarry Bank in 1955 to be a midwife, when Nurse Green retired. At the time there was no clinic, and therefore prospective mothers had to come to Jessie's house in Bobs Coppice on Wednesday afternoons to book her services. Eventually a clinic did open in Brierley Hill.

As a result of Local Government changes in 1966, Nurse Gullick went to work in Wordsley Hospital, but she continues to live in her adopted home of Quarry Bank. Her skills and caring approach are still remembered, so she is still often greeted in Quarry Bank as "Nurse Gullick".

Delivering Pop

Dan Plant started on his own in 1948. First he sold bags of logs and bundles of firewood, and then gradually he began selling mineral waters, or "pop" to the locals. At first he sold Shaw's drinks, bottled in Merry Hill, then he moved on to Tizer, Green's and Corona. Then he also began to sell groceries.

Dan Plant's round covered most of Quarry Bank, as well as travelling further afield to Kingswinford, Pensnett, Stourbridge, Oldswinford and Norton - giving service to many people who became good friends.

The Plants lived in Merry Hill and then moved to Amblecote Road where they carried on until they retired in 1979. It was a small family firm - helped out by a young lad named Jack Cartwright on Saturdays and holidays. Dan Plant's son moved on to other things in 1968, however Grandson Stephen used to help the Plants as he grew up and became known among his friends as "Danny".

Delivering the Milk

Robert Chance of Freehold farm (See page 13) is seen here delivering milk with Dolly in the early 1970s.

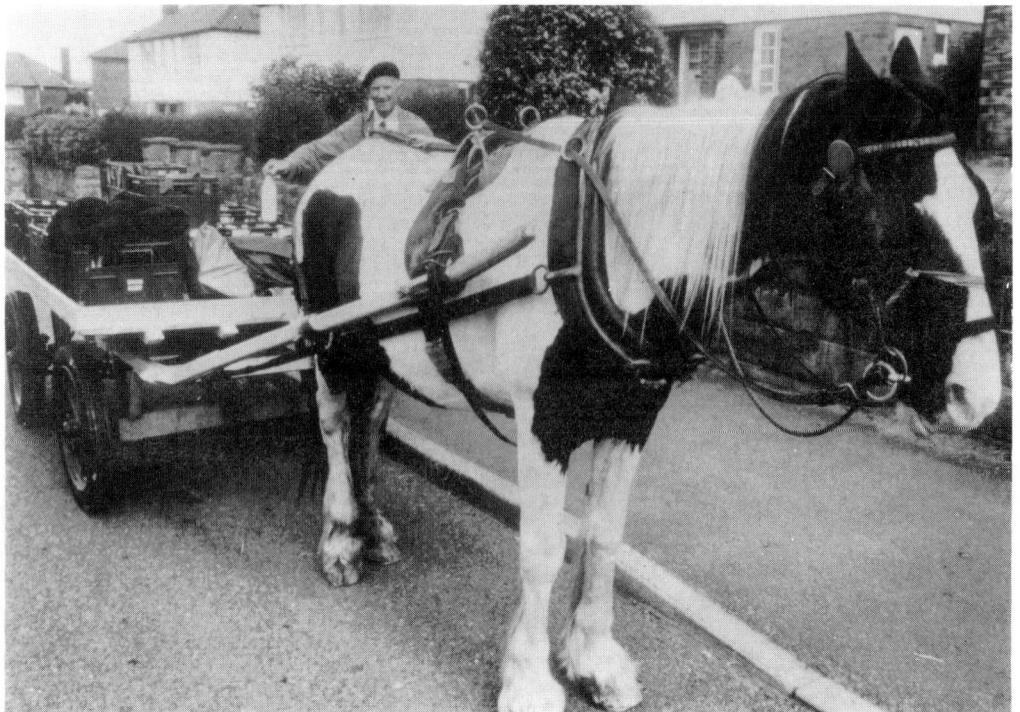

Working at Malin's

Malin's originally came from Birmingham, and moved into the premises in Thorns Road about 1962. The firm was run by Mr. Geoff Malin and his two sons, Eric and Steven. The building had originally been part of a brick works on the site and, at that time, the stack was still standing. Malin's gradually extended the building and adapted it for their purposes.

Malin's were manufacturers of the famous "Mamod" miniature steam engines which had remained unchanged for years - but now the firm wanted to extend and improve the range and eventually introduced miniature live steam railway locomotives and accessories.

The firm brought many of the Birmingham staff to their new works and there was some degree of rivalry between the Brummies and the Quarry Bankers but this was soon forgotten in the happy and friendly atmosphere that prevailed. The staff enjoyed Summer Outings and a Christmas Social that was usually held in Birmingham. Things did not go well for the live steam model railway system and even launching a set to mark the wedding of Charles and Diana did little to save the product. Dave Evans, the manager, decided to improve production with the introduction of new machines, but it was too late, and the firm was eventually sold to a Mr. Cooper who moved production to the South of England in the 1980s.

Top left: Betty Hadlington on the press.
Top right: Elsie Jackson on the press.
Bottom Left: Hilda Perry, Elsie Jackson, Ada James and May Price.
Bottom Right: Bert Watkiss, Jack Edwards, Ron Butler.
(Photos from Betty Hadlington's Collection)

A Norman Edwards cartoon round-up of the staff at B.H.Castings Ltd.

Above: Eric Attwood - the last Quarry Bank chain maker to continue working on his own hearth at the back of his home. Eric made chain for fifty years and the hearth at the back of his home in Brick Kiln Street was still being used in the 1970s.

Many names associated with Quarry Bank's holloware trade have disappeared but Bird Stevens & Co. still occupy a prominent position between Merry Hill and Sun Street. Robert Stevens and William Bird began trading as galvanised holloware manufacturers in 1913. The firm has changed hands a few times, and has survived by adopting new materials, and producing a new wide range of products.

Right: Bird Stevens works as seen from Merry Hill in May 1998.

Chapter 6
Murder in Quarry Bank

(Researched by Patrick & Sylvia Shaw, with additional information from Jack Beddall)

In the early hours of 10th March 1856 fifteen year old Thomas Brown was returning home with his parents. As he approached the New Inn in Quarry Bank High Street he saw a man lying in the road face upwards and motionless. He took the man's hand and found it was cold. Thomas's parents joined him and announced that the man must be dead, and sent their son to summon the landlord of The New Inn, and the police.

The corpse was 20 year old David Taylor a local horse-nail maker, and when P.C. Millington arrived and started to examine the body it was soon obvious that Taylor had been killed. He had a stab wound in his chest, there was blood on the ground, and other minor wounds that suggested a fight had taken place. The body was taken to The New Inn, where an inquest was eventually held.

By the time P.C. Millington had moved the body to the New Inn, information about the circumstances of Taylor's death was coming to light, and the constable had no hesitation in proceeding to the home of a Joseph Chivers and apprehending him on a charge of causing an affray and causing David Taylor's death. Joseph Chivers was taken to Brierley Hill and put in custody.

The inquest took place in two parts as the first session at the New Inn was followed by another session at the Royal Oak. At the latter the jury decided that Joseph Chivers had murdered David Taylor and should be sent for trial. The events that had led to Taylor's death had been fairly brief, but were complicated enough to cast some doubt on whether it was "murder" or "manslaughter". Taylor had been returning to Quarry Bank with some pals. The fight had started after Chivers, plus his father and brother had complained that their cart had been interfered with. The central question seemed to be whether Chivers had acted in a moment of passion or whether the incident had lasted long enough for him to have acted in a more considered way. Witnesses tended to provide a picture of quite a prolonged fight in which Chivers gained the upper hand, and once Taylor was on the ground had plenty of time to withdraw from the situation, but in fact had continued to attack Taylor while on the ground and while stating that he intended to kill him.

Joseph Chivers was brought to trial in July 1856, before Mr. Justice Wightman. Several things were said in defence of Chivers and the jury decided that he acted without premeditated malice and was therefore guilty of manslaughter. The Judge was of the opinion that it was "very little short of murder" and Chivers was sentenced to fifteen years transportation.

Quarry Bank's other "famous" murder occurred in 1906 in a cottage behind the Fountain Inn, at 18 Victoria Street. At the time the cottage was occupied by Edmund Clarke, his wife and children, and his father-in-law, Joseph Jones. The cottage had once belonged to the latter but it had been transferred to Mr. Clarke, after which there appears to have been continual ill-feeling between the two men.

On the evening of Saturday 1st December 1906 Mrs. Clarke had left her husband asleep in the divided living room of the cottage while she went to the shops. When she returned, at about 9.00 pm., her father let her in. She found Edmund "sitting" on the sofa, covered in blood. She turned to her father and said, "What have you done this for?" He is said to have replied, "Because he started on me," and then left the premises.

Mrs. Clarke summoned neighbours for help, but nothing could be done to save Edmund, although he was still alive at that time. His head had been struck and his throat had been cut. PC Jones dealt with matters at the scene of the crime - which was soon the centre of considerable "public interest". A PC Maisey accompanied Joseph Jones back to the cottage after meeting him in Quarry Bank and hearing him confess to having hit his son-in-law with a poker. Joseph was calm throughout the incident, and when remanded, slept peacefully at Brierley Hill Police Station.

Edmund Clarke had died at the age of twenty eight, and his funeral took place on 8th December. He had been a chain-maker and haulier by trade and a popular Sunday School teacher. The procession therefore was led by Rev. McNulty with the church heavily represented. Everyone spoke of his quiet disposition and high moral character. Friends established a fund for the widow and her three sons. Joseph Jones, meanwhile, was charged with murder.

Joseph Jones' trial took place in March 1907 at Stafford Assizes. The Defence tried to argue that Joseph had been provoked and the counter attack was not wilful, and therefore it was a case of manslaughter. The jury was not convinced and took only twenty five minutes to reach the conclusion that he was guilty of murder. Joseph Jones was sentenced to death by hanging. Shortly before his execution Joseph wrote a lengthy letter to William Hayes, the landlord of the Church Tavern, insisting that his version of events was the truth and that he had been much provoked by his son-in-law.

Left: James Henry Paskin's shop is described as a General Draper and Gents Tailor at 27 High Street. The lady by the door is probably Mrs. Astley - the grandmother of Paskin Astley who played for England Schoolboys against Wales in 1927.
Mr. & Mrs. Paskin also kept the Vine Inn at the corner of Victoria Road.
The picture dates from about 1910, and the premises today are occupied by Firkin's Bakery.
(Photo from Ivy Astley)

Left: Yates' Stores
Robert Yates in the doorway, his wife Alice, on the right.
(Margaret Yates' Collection)

Left: Crocko's Shop,in the Lower High Street.
Photographed by John James in the early 1960s.

Chapter 7
Quarry Bank Shops

On many occasions at the Mount Pleasant Local History Group we have found ourselves talking about the shops. Just the names of local shops prompt strong memories, and, of course, shops themselves are always changing, as if to remind us that nothing ever stays the same for long - even in Quarry Bank! Our discussions have often taken us on journeys down the High Street or along Mount Pleasant - trying to recreate the correct sequence of shops and their history. This is not as easy as it sounds because our memories may belong to different periods. One shop stays the same while its neighbour changes, and very soon our stories are over-lapping and becoming confused.

The general picture that emerges is that even in a town the size of Quarry Bank there were once many shops, many of which must have served a very local clientele. General stores existed in many of the side streets and the High Street was a thriving bustling commercial centre. The fact that people are now much more mobile and go further afield to meet their shopping needs, plus the trend towards one-stop supermarket shopping, has changed everything. And having one of Europe's largest shopping complexes as your next door neighbour tends to have an effect on local shopping!

We begin this section by trying to provide a description of the shops in Quarry Bank's High Street - based on the scene described by Sue Smith, recalling the late 1950s. These notes have been augmented by information collected by Joan Pearson and other members of the group, and we have included reference to the current use of these buildings to try and help the reader keep his or her bearings!

A Journey down the High Street

As recalled by **Sue Smith** - remembering the scene towards the end of the 1950s, and augmented by notes made by **Joan Pearson and others.**

Our journey begins at The Blue Ball and proceeds down the High Street - first of all sticking to the left hand side, and then making our way down the right hand side:

The old Blue Ball was demolished in the 1960s and was replaced with the present building, but the houses below the Blue Ball have remained remarkably unchanged. (Note - see picture on page 10 of QBiOP, revealing that small shops had once been provided in 6, 7 and 8 High Street.). The first shop encountered in the late 1950s was in the third building down from Sun Street - a grocery shop owned by Miss Dwyer. As the High Street bends towards Oak Street we came across the Salisbury Buildings of 1892 vintage, 17 - 19 High Street, demolished in 1998 to make way for the new road system. At no. 18 was the Valeting Service and on the corner was the bike shop.

On the other corner of Oak Street was the Royal Oak - now replaced with more modern buildings, the first of which is occupied by Take a Bite. Originally these premises were followed by Hill's Furniture shop and then Marsh & Baxters, which had once been Bird's Butchers shop. Then came the dry-cleaners, which is now Harry Scrivens' shop at 25 High Street. In the late 1950s one then came to Hayne's shop at 27 High Street. (This is the shop seen at the top of the page opposite when it was run by Henry James Paskin.) Mrs. Haynes sold paraffin, candles, soap, fireworks and light bulbs etc... Later it was acquired by Robinson's Bakery and they, in turn, were taken over, in 1982, by Firkins' Bakery who still reside in the shop today.

Left: No.27 High Street down to the Conservative Club - as it was in the 1970s. (Dave Whyley)

Next door was Guests' fruit and veg, run by two sisters. The shop is now closed, but it was last used as a fruit and veg shop known as Knowle's. Then came Pat Bostock's shop, trading simply as "Pat's", which sold general household goods and grocery. Now it is a solicitor's, before it was Pat's it was a cafe.

At 29 High Street we come to the Conservative Club, which has changed very little over the years, but the buildings next door have been demolished to provide access to the club's carpark. Once there had been a bowling green at the back of the club. What is now Bertie's Sandwich Shop and cafe was once a house and sweet shop, and the Indian "take-away" on the corner of Church Street was Homer's - then taken over by Taylor's. Homer's also ran coaches, which were kept in Park Road. Homer's was a double-fronted shop, one side selling groceries, the other side a drapers. (The complete row of buildings from Oak Street to Church Street as they were in the 1900s can be seen on page of 13 of QBiOP.)

The Church Tavern features in many pictures of Quarry Bank High Street. It has changed name a few times recently and is now "The Nailmaker", but many people still refer to it by its old name. Next door to The Church Tavern was Sally Wasdell's pharmacy, which is described in more detail below. Sally extended her shop into the premises next door, which had once been Wootton's shoe shop. 39 and 40 High Street were originally cottages built well back from the current building line. They were converted into shops by extending the ground floor forwards to a shop front. In the 1950s they were occupied by Stringer's radio and electrical stores and by Rock's fruit and wet fish shop. Now they have become The Cottage Surgery and people come from miles around to use the high-tech tattoo removal service provided in these premises.

The building which now houses Quarry Bank's Post Office is quite an impressive three storey building built at a slight angle to the general building line, once again suggesting that the buildings in this stretch pre-date the more formal laying out of the line of the High Street in the 1880s. In the 1950s it was Hill's Furniture shop and it later became Bennett's newsagents.

The prevailing building line is restored as we reach 44/45 High Street, which is now a Balti Restaurant. In the 1930s we would have found Evelyn Foxall's sweet shop at no. 44 in a style matching no. 48 (See QBiOP page 90), but in the 1950s we would have found Evelyn Chuter's grocery and then another fruit and veg shop. 46/47 was an electrical goods shop which is now Homer's. We then come to a pair of old shops separated by an entry which belonged to the Kendall family. The first, no. 48 was Kendall's wine shop, and it is still a wine shop today. It had once been the location of Quarry Bank Post Office - run by a Mr. Griffiths. Then it became a wine merchant's shop run by Clifford Adolphus Hawkeswood. He was an accomplished church organist at a Stourbridge church, and relief organist at Quarry Bank.

Next door Kendall's sold general household goods, furnishings, toys and fireworks. Its classical late Victorian shop front has survived well, with its attractive leaded glass quarter lights and glazed brick wall beneath the window. The pilasters and even the door have not yet been "modernised", and the premises are currently occupied by "Betty's Stitch Kits". Next door, The Vine Inn became a Dental Laboratory with an extended and prominent frontage, but even that is currently "For Sale". It stands on the corner of Victoria Road, beyond which the gradient of the High Street begins to increase.

On the lower corner of Victoria Road was a branch of the Brierley Hill & Stourbridge Building Society - now "Creations" - then a grocery shop which has now returned to residential use. Then came the shop that had been Sally Wasdell's first premises. This later became A & S Television Services, but is now Cash Weighing Systems. There is a very small shop at 55 High Street,

Left: Sally Wasdell's shop in the 1950s - before it extended into the premises next door, which at this time was a shoe shop. (Bill Bawden)

Above: Sally Wasdell in her car, with Gladys Hall and a visiting French teacher who was staying with Sally at the time. (Collection of Gladys Hall)

Today's Post Office is located centrally in the premises of Guys' newsagents, confectioners & tobacconists. (Ned Williams)

Right: Stringers electrical goods shop and the fruit and veg shop in the 1970s, which are now Dr. Rigler's Cottage Surgery. (Dave Whyley)

Bottom left: This little grocery shop, once Foster's, has now closed and the building is residential again. (Dave Whyley)

Bottom Right: Kendall's shop at 49 High Street in the mid 1970s. (Dave Whyley)

33

This striking postcard view of Quarry Bank High Street in the "Landscape View" series illustrates the shops from Oak Street down to Kendall's in the 1950s.

(Ken Rock Collection)

which now houses Festival Computing, beyond which the building line is again interrupted by no. 56. which is built an imposing angle to the street. No. 56 was once Groves, the butchers. The business was started sometime in the 1880s by Walter Grove, followed by his son Stan, and then Stan's son, Raymond. It went out of the Grove family's possession in 1968 and is now A. Jewess. Outside the shop was the big tree which marked the beginning of the steep descent to the lower end of the High Street. This tree can just be seen in various old photographs of Quarry Bank High Street - as seen on the cover of this book!

The stretch from 57 to 63 High Street formed part of the Sheffield Street community and consisted of old residential properties that were demolished to create a space on which the Community Centre could be built. (This story is told later.)

On the steep descent below Sheffield Street we find some imposing buildings - nos. 64/65/66 being solid late Victorian or early Edwardian buildings, followed by 67/69, being a more modern inter-war structure that may well have replaced three older buildings. The corner shop at 64 was the booking office for Genner's Coaches, 65 was Genner's fish and chip shop, later known as "The Fryery". Today 64 and 65 have been knocked into one larger fish and chip shop. At 66, what had been Bruton's grocery, is no longer in use. (In the 1930s it had been William Bucknall's sweets and grocery shop.)The 1930s building next door features a residential section (67) plus an attractive shop front which had once been a Betting Office, but which is not currently in commercial use.

From this point onwards the Quarry Bank Primary School's property faces the High Street, with a very attractive caretaker's lodge at no. 71. By popping into the school entrance it is possible to see Genner's former coach garage at the back of their High Street premises - with name "Sunridge Coaches" still just visible on the gable end. Beyond the school was Price's sweet shop, now a hairdresser trading as   "Jeanette & Wendy" in the 1970s, now trading as "Heroes".

In the 1950s Thompson's shoe repair shop was next to Price's, but this has now been the Tin Sing Chinese food "takeaway" for many years. Next door was a chemist shop which is now another hairdresser, followed by 80 to 83 High Street, taking us down to the Queens Head, which was demolished in the 1970s. Adjacent to the Queens Head was Shaw Brothers - builders and painters & decorators and a couple of small dwellings. Beyond these was a small garage - "J.G. Motors" - which grew into QB Bikes and moved further down the road, into what had been The Elephant & Castle on the corner of Rose Hill.

Like Sheffield Street, this is an area of very early development of urban Quarry Bank - beyond which there were fields and small holdings of rural Quarry Bank descending into the valley of the Mousesweet Brook. One such field was used to provide space to build the Coronet Cinema in the 1930s, and other fields disappeared beneath the Woodland Avenue Estate. Urban Quarry Bank extended a little further on the other side of the High Street, as we shall see.

Right: A mid 1970s view of Quarry Bank High Street, between Victoria Road and Sheffield Street. The tree that was once such a well-known landmark in the High Street was just to the right of this view.

(John James)

Right: The shop occupied by A. Jewess in the above picture can be seen here in the early days when run by the Grove Family. Note the ornamental ox-head on the pillar on the left.

(June Grove's Collection)

Below: Looking into the Lower High Street in the mid 1970s. The original Quarry Bank School is prominent, and there seems to be less traffic than there is today! (Note the buildings just beyond the school and compare them with the picture overleaf.)

35

Left: A post card from Frank Webb's collection on which he has marked the position on which the 'second' land mine fell in 1940. The building was built by his father, and in this pre-war view was occupied by E. Sheldon (printer) and the Quarry Bank Coffee House. The oriel window can be seen in the picture at the foot of the previous page, but the arched-bay on the ground floor was altered after the war.

To make our way down the right hand side of the High Street (the "south" side) we must go back to The Blue Ball and begin the journey all over again. The stretch from Thorns Road to the Sun Inn was still fields at the beginning of the century, but is now occupied by inter-war houses built by Frank Webb - including his own house at Hillcroft. The Sun Inn also appears to have been rebuilt between the wars, and occupies the spot where the old High Street begins to bend. On this bend we once came to Hawkswood's iron-mongers shop, at 212 High Street.

Hawkswood's were an old firm of nail foggers and dealers in blacksmithing iron, horse shoes, provender merchants etc., the family being well-established in Quarry Bank in its "formative" years. Mr. Hawkeswood ran the business with his sons Herbert and Fred. Herbert travelled as far afield as Wales while selling the iron, while Fred served in the shop. Before the First World War, Herbert's journeys were undertaken in a pony and trap. They had once supplied iron to the local nailmakers hence the term 'nail foggers' - and the nailers then brought the finished nails back to be sold in the shop.

Hawkeswoods installed what appears to have been the first petrol pump in Quarry Bank in the 1930s, and installed electric light in their cellar. The original 1920s electric light bulb was still working, although only with a glimmer, when the business was sold in the late 1960s. Mr. King, the new owner, kept various records to put on show in the shop - including log book and invoices written in copper-plate by Herbert Hawkeswood. The premises are now Jantino's bridal-wear shop.

Stretching from Hawkswood's towards the corner of Park Road were some tenement properties known as "The High Buildings", or "Bird's Buildings". These were demolished at the end of 1967, and the corner is now occupied by a small car-park facing the recently re-aligned High Street. We don't encounter further shops on this side of the High Street until we have passed Christ Church and the Library. Retail premises run from 196 (now the Halifax Building Society/Chell's Insurance Broking) to the corner of Chapel Street (formerly Z Street). The corner, now Dave Evans' electrical repair shop, was another location used as Quarry Bank Post Office before moving across the road to the present site.

On the other corner of Chapel Street was the Co-op. The story of the Co-op is told in more detail below. Today it is the MS Supermarket. Next door to the Co-op at 192 was a small building which is currently Vicky's Pet Grooming Parlour. Then came the Midland Bank - now Cloud Nine Balloons - and the Betting Office, now run by Wilf Gilbert.

Next door to the Betting Office is a Beauty Parlour/hairdressers now trading as "Shades". Then came Thomas' butcher's shop, at 187, with a slaughter-house behind the premises. Charles Thomas' shop was taken over by his son George and then passed to Charles' nephew - Harry Thomas. This area is now occupied by a Tandoori Restaurant, neighbouring the Congregational Church. The Sunday School hall next to the church was opened in 1967, and must have been built on land formerly occupied by shops at 182-185 High Street, one of which was a shoe shop in the 1950s.

Below the Congregational Church was a paint and wallpaper shop which is now a dental surgery. Then came Briscoe's grocery, Wallin's shoe shop, and Knot's butchers shop. All three premises have now become Hawthorn & Walker's, the butchers. There is a small gap at this point before buildings resume, therefore making the drapers shop at 172 seem like a corner shop. It is now Beverley's Pet Food Store. Small shops now descend the steep part of the High Street, opposite the Community Centre and Sheffield Street, down to the New Inns. The buildings are smaller and seem more representative of the world of lower High Street.

Right: Hawkswood's shop is seen just beyond the 'High Buildings' in an Edwardian post card view of the top of Quarry Bank High Street. (Detail from Beech card in the collection of Frank Webb)

Right: The Hawkeswood Family. (Frank Webb Collection)

Below: The shops just across the High Street from the junction with Sheffield Street in the 1970s.
Freddie Field's "Central Hairdressing". Malcolm Bennet's shop is now the pet shop. (Dave Whyley)

Once there was a small fruit and veg shop, The Central Hairdressers, Tipton's drapers (Formerly Glaze's -see QBiOP page 20), another hairdressers, and then the New Inn. Today there are still hairdressers in this stretch.

The New Inn is on the corner of Queen Street, and the area south of the High Street from here onwards is representative of Quarry Bank's late Victorian expansion. Queen Street, Maughan Street and New Street, were presumably laid out by the District Road Board of the 1880s. On the lower side of Queen Street we come to "Ingleside" dated 1900. This was the famous surgery of Dr. Maylett Smith, immortalised in *"A GP's Progress to the Black Country"*, and is still in use as a Medical Centre.

Next door to Ingleside was MacDonald's fruit and veg shop, now Tina's soft furnishings, followed by Taylor's grocery and sweet shop, now a laundry. Today we come across James Hadley's Antiques and the Wear & Tear upholstery shop that had once been Guilder's grocery. There was a dry-cleaners shop which is now in residential use, followed by Price's (the painters and decorators) and then Thompson's - a soft furnishings shop run by Ann Thompson and a cobblers run by Cecil. This is now the carpet shop trading as "Walter Wall". This brings us to the Liberal Club.

Beyond the Liberal Club and The Labour Club we are very much in Lower Quarry Bank, descending towards the junction with New Street. Before reaching New Street we would once have passed a wet fish shop, a fish and chip shop (Our Plaice),and another hairdressers and barbers shop. On the lower corner of New Street was Yates' Grocery, followed by a terrace of very solid Victorian houses with imposing lintels above the windows. Just before reaching The Three Horse Shoes was a wood shop. The Three Horse Shoes has now been demolished.

If you have found this trip round the shops in the High Street exhausting, don't forget there were many other shops in Quarry Bank! New Street had many shops, Mount Pleasant had its own shops, as well as the shops where Thorns Road ran into Merry Hill. Many other side roads and "suburbs" were served by their local general stores, some of which still exist.

Left: The Liberal Club, and Walter Wall's carpet shop - which had once been Ann and Cecil Thompson's shops. Feb. 1998 . (Ned Williams)

Above: S.Street's shop, Lower High Street.

Above: Granny Bloomer's Shop

DORIS M. COX

The General Stores at 53 New Street

Information gathered by **Horace Dunn**

Doris Cox was born in Hayes Lane in 1907, and after working at Cradley Printing Co., went to work for her uncle, Albert Ketley, working on spades and shovels. Her Aunt Polly kept the shop which was at the front of the works. Doris found herself looking after the shop when her Aunt and Uncle had a few days off, and she finally took it over when they retired. This meant that the shop was kept in the family for over 80 years. Doris built up a reputation for the best ham around, and the children loved her "cherry lips" and "Kayli".

Doris Cox's shop was open long hours and only closed for bank holidays, and Doris was not able to retire until 1975 - after having worked in the shop for forty one years. Louie Potts and Alice Stamford helped in the shop, plus Beryl Kirkham, and much later Brenda Holloway.

Doris' husband, Christopher Cox, who also worked for Uncle Albert, later became the President of the Liberal Club, and was greatly respected.

Below: Doris outside the shop in 1975 - retiring at the age of 68. The shop has now been altered into residential premises.

SALLY WASDELL

These notes on Sally Wasdell's shop were written after **Gladys Hall** visited the History Group to talk about working for Sally. Gladys worked for Sally from the age of fifteen until she retired at the age of fifty eight. She began working as an assistant but was taught dispensing by Sally.

Sally Wasdell was born in Cradley Heath or Old Hill about 1887/8 and was one of five children. She began her working life with Dr. Tibbetts of Cradley Heath and trained as a dispenser, then as a fully qualified pharmacist. She opened her shop in Quarry Bank High Street - opposite the church gates - in premises that had been well known as a greengrocers shop. She also qualified as an optician (FBOA) and was highly regarded in this kind of work. She was a founder member of the Dudley Branch of the Pharmaceutical Society and became its first lady President - possibly the only lady to hold that office.

In the 1950s Miss Wasdell was able to buy no. 53 High Street, after the death of a Mr.Edmund who had been in charge of Cox's drug-wholesaling business. She also bought a house in Stourbridge in which she opened another optical department. She made her home in Barber House - a house built by Frank Webb at the top of the High Street.

Sally was well-known in Quarry Bank and everyone knew her old Austin, later a Morris Minor, and her two Scottie dogs. She was bedridden for the last couple of years of her life but her mind was active and she kept the business going and maintained daily contact with the shops. A Jack Attwood bought the shop and continued to trade as Sally Wasdell - Jack's wife was a pharmacist. He extended the business into what had been Wootton's Shoe Shop next door - and the premises are still occupied by a pharmacy today.

Sally Wasdell died on 3 September 1959 at the age of 72 and is buried in the Victoria Road Cemetery.

The Co-op.

Nobody seems certain when the Dudley Co-operative Society opened its branch in Quarry Bank. (I guess the Co-op came to Quarry Bank in the late 1880s or early 1890s.) It was certainly open in 1904 because we know that in that year Mary Ann Hadlington came to work there as the 21 year old manageress. (It was rare in the 1900s for the Co-op to appoint a woman to manage a branch so she must have impressed the Society in the previous seven years that she had worked for them after leaving school.)

Ten years after starting work at Quarry Bank Co-op Mary married Joe Marsh who had also worked for the Co-op from about 1910 onwards when he had left school. Mary Marsh, as she now was, pushed Co-op membership and made Quarry Bank a flourishing part of the Dudley Society. She was also very active in the life of the church and had been a Sunday School Teacher.

Everyone was very shocked when she died on 27th December 1927 at the early age of 44. There was a huge turnout for her funeral from family, friends, officials of the Society, and of Quarry Bankers in the Society. She was buried in Quarry Bank churchyard.

Joe was appointed in her place as Manager of the shop - which again must have been fairly unusual as very few husbands can have followed their wives in managing a Co-op branch. In 1960, while celebrating fifty years of service to the Co-op, Joe Marsh came to the public's attention by saving a ten year old girl from drowning on the South Devon coast. He was commended by the Society and by Stan Hill of Brierley Hill UDC - now better known as the editor of the Blackcountryman magazine. It is assumed that Joe retired five years later in 1965.

Above: Joe Marsh - Manager of the Quarry Bank Branch of the Co-op. (From the collection of Mrs. Marsh)

The Dudley Co-operative Society was absorbed by the Greater Midlands Society, based in Birmingham, in 1982. At the time, the Quarry Bank Branch was regarded as profitable and therefore worth saving, but it was not long before the GMCS pulled out of Dudley altogether, and the shop was sold.

Right: MS Supermarket now occupies the building which was once the local branch of the Dudley Co-operative Society.
Feb. 1998 (Ned Williams)

40

Chapter 8
The Churches of Quarry Bank

A general outline of the history of the churches in Quarry Bank was published in "Quarry Bank in Old Photographs", so this chapter is not going to repeat that material. We include here one or two written and pictorial items that relate to Quarry Bank's churches that have come to light since the publication of that book.

The Parish Church:
Christ Church, Quarry Bank.

The Day the Church Caught Fire.

On Sunday 12th November 1900 Christ Church Quarry Bank was heated for the Evening Service in the usual manner. The heating apparatus was in a chamber directly beneath the vestry floor at the southern side of the chancel. There was no brick arch separating the boiler from the wooden floor of the vestry, but that was something that was taken for granted and gave no one any cause for concern when the boiler was refuelled at about 5.00 pm.

It was about nine o'clock, after the evening service when the Vicar, Rev. McNulty, and the Sexton left the vestry to return home. The vicarage is not far from the church and Miss McNulty's bedroom overlooked its eastern flank. About 2 o'clock in the morning she was awoken by crackling noises and saw flashing light coming from the vestry. At about the same time, P.C. Lawson of Quarry Bank Police Station became aware that there was a fire somewhere in the vicinity of the church. He rushed to the church and then on to the vicarage, arriving there just as Rev. McNulty was hurriedly dressing to investigate what was going on.

They found the fire had gained a hold in the vestry and P.C. Lawson rushed to the homes of the church wardens, William Dudley and Joseph Raybould to summon their assistance while the Vicar rang the church bell. Everybody grabbed a bucket, filled it with water from a tap in the churchyard and poured water into the vestry. This had little effect and it was soon obvious that the fire had now spread from the floor to the ceiling and roof timbers. Someone suggested summoning the Fire Brigade from Brierley Hill Police Station by telephoning from a nearby shop. Everybody present continued to fight the fire thinking that someone else had followed up this suggestion - then they realised that nobody had done so! Joseph Raybould's son had, however, set off for Brierley Hill on foot, followed by Frank Hawkeswood on horseback! The alarm was sounded at Brierley Hill at 3.00 am.

Lieutenants Charlton and Baker, plus eight men were heading for Quarry Bank within a quarter of an hour with a manual pump. When they arrived they found there was no fire hydrant in Quarry Bank. They attached a standpipe but found that their master key would not open the valve. They had to send for the Council Surveyor, Mr. J.T. Abbiss, who produced a key which also turned out to be ineffective! Someone from the water company was summoned but enjoyed no success. The Fire Brigade were frantic to find an adequate supply of water and the water company employee was able to take them to an overflow "wash out" in Bower Lane. This enabled the firefighters to reach a water supply and soon the hoses were in position and the pump was in action.

As the powerful jet of water was projected at the vestry it became obvious that almost everything had been consumed by the fire by that time, and that the fire was about to spread to the main building of the church. However, water had arrived just in time to save the main structure of the church and the fire was quickly brought under control. The pew-ends were scorched and the recently decorated interior was smoke-damaged, but the chancel had been saved. A non fire-proof safe kept in the vestry had just about survived with minimal damage to its contents - partly melted communion plate and singed vestry records. Everything else had gone.

Rev. McNulty hoped that insurance would cover the cost of putting things right, but the event caused much local discussion about the lack of hydrants. The Urban District Council complained that the Local Government Board had refused to make loans available for Quarry Bank to purchase hydrants and was quibbling over the precise positioning of such hydrants. Although much was said about the time it took to bring the fire under control, Rev. McNulty seemed to feel grateful that the main structure of the church itself was saved - "just in time".

Mount Pleasant Methodist Church

The Wesleyan church in Mount Pleasant celebrated its 170th anniversary in 1998 and a review of its history was printed to mark the event. The previous attempt to tell the church's story had been made at the centenary in 1928, just after the church had been considerably rebuilt and improved. Ernest Stevens was frequently the benefactor in the case of Mount Pleasant Church as his wife Mary had been an active member of its congregation.

Like all Quarry Bank churches, Mount Pleasant's history includes stories of Sunday Schools, football teams and youth clubs, choirs and dramatic activities. One interesting wartime event organised for the youth of the church was a "mock wedding" in which all the males were females and vice versa!

The Sunday School building behind the church was a pleasant brick and terracotta structure of 1902 vintage and much work was done on this building in the 1980s only to be defeated by the arrival of dry rot. In the end the building was demolished and the 1990s have been spent in upgrading the church itself and making it more of a multi-purpose building.

Above Right: The church in Mount Pleasant.

Right: Mount Pleasant Church in 1978. The exterior of the church received attention in 1975 and work then began on the interior in time for its 150th anniversary.

(Olive Allchurch)

The Primitive Methodist Church
New Street

Methodist Chapels had existed in Quarry Bank from 1830 onwards, and the first chapel in New Street was built in 1860. The building was replaced and enlarged as the congregation grew, but suffered a setback in 1897 when it was destroyed by mining subsidence - a reminder of how close mining came to the centre of Quarry Bank. The final New Street chapel was opened in 1903 and lasted until 1981.

After the First World War, the church built up a very flourishing Sunday School - with a Sunday afternoon attendance of about 380! This led to the usual youth activities and football teams. At one stage the trustees of the church bought an old Army hut, put it up next to the Sunday School room and opened it as a Young People's Social Institute.

*Top right: The "last wedding" conducted at New Street Methodist Church - on 30th December 1979.
The preacher is S. Hills, the organist is Arthur Bird BEM.
(Julie Dunn Colln.)*

*Right: A postcard view of New Street showing the chapel, next door to Edwin Cox's chemist shop.
(Jack Beddall Colln.)*

*Right: the Primitive Methodists Football Team in 1920/21. Back row: Arthur Bird, Lol Dudley, Sam Darby. Middle row: Ernest Bloomer, George Penn, Sid Jones, George Maybury, Baden Sidaway, William Bridgwater. Front row: Lawson Thompson, Alf Yardley, Ralph Allport, Frank Maley, Jim Stringer.
(Julie Dunn Colln.)*

Cradley Forge Methodist Church
Hammer Bank

The History of Methodism in the Cradley Forge area is very complicated, but the chapel in use today was built in 1928 as a Sunday School building and became the church itself when the building at the foot of the bank was closed and demolished in 1938. Once again there is a story of Sunday Schools, social and sporting activities, etc., but the most famous activity to emerge from Cradley Forge was the musical adventure which led to the formation of the Operatic & Dramatic Society.

Above: The church today

Left: The ladies of Cradley Forge take a charabanc trip in 1926.
  (Margaret Yates Collection)

Below: Cradley Forge Sunday School Football team, 1923/24.
(J. Mason Collection)

Birch Coppice Methodist Church - Coppice Lane

Right: A Primitive Methodist chapel was built in Coppice Lane in the mid 1880s, and was replaced by this corrugated iron building towards the end of that decade. Not many "tin chapels" have survived, and this one was replaced by the brick building seen below in 1958. ·

Right: The new brick building at Church Coppice is seen here on the day that it opened - 23rd August 1958.
Some modifications have since been made to the porch.

Right: The Birch Coppice Methodist Church Sunday School teachers of 1958.
S. Monkton, Mr, & Mrs. J Woodhouse, Mrs. M. Price, Rev. Clemitson, Miss B. Dunn, Mrs. N. Delley, Mr. R. Sidaway, Mrs. G. Dudley, Miss I. Forrest, Mrs. G. Smith, Mrs. A. Jones, Mrs. E Flohr, Mrs. E. Raybould, Mrs. M Rousell, Mrs. F. Clift.

(This page was compiled with the help of Joy Woodhouse and Mary Rousell.)

The Congregational Church
High Street

The Congregational Church, opened in 1935, and the Sunday School building, opened in 1967, stand alongside each other in Quarry Bank High Street.

Left: The present building replaced the old "Z Street Mission" of 1897 vintage. Photographed in 1967, just before demolition, by Alan Southall.

Left: Crowds flock into the new Sunday School in 1967. Just beyond the new building it is possible to see the roof of the rear portion of the redundant Z Street building. (Z Street is now called Chapel Street.)
(Alan Southall)

Chapter 9
Quarry Bank School Days

The development of Education in Quarry Bank follows a pattern seen in most towns of the Black County. The earliest efforts directed towards providing some schooling were made in poorly documented "dame schools", followed quickly by "National" schools established under the wing of the Church of England. (Quarry Bank's "National & Parochial School" opened at the beginning of 1866 and struggled to educate its unruly pupils.)

The Education Act of 1870 was the "turning point" which established the concept of universal education, and set up the local School Boards to organise its proviso. Quarry Bank found itself in the large area covered by the Kingswinford School Board, and its first two schools were built by the board. The first was the Quarry Bank school which opened in Lower High Street in 1872, and the second was the Mount Pleasant School which opened ten years later, but did not move into its purpose built buildings until 1888. The original primary school in the High Street expanded over the years and was replaced in 1937 by the large two-storey building in use today.

Eventually the role of the School Boards was taken on by the Education Committees of the County Councils, and Quarry Bank came under the wing of the South West Division of Staffordshire. Secondary Education was not forced upon children until the "leaving age" crept up towards 14 and the provision of school places had to be expanded. It was 1932 when the Secondary Schools opened in new purpose-built buildings in Coppice Lane.

The reorganisation of Secondary Education following the 1944 Education Act did not result in either a Grammar School or a Technical School being built in Quarry Bank. The school-leaving age crept up to 15, and local pupils who had shown academic aptitude in their 11+ had to leave the town to pursue Secondary Education of the Grammar School type. With hindsight we can see that Quarry Bank would have been just the right size to have a Comprehensive School of the type pioneered by the South West Division of Staffordshire in the 1950s, but it was 1975 before such an idea became a reality in Quarry Bank - by which time the schools of the town were part of Dudley County Borough's system.

As Quarry Bank expanded in the 1960s an additional primary school became necessary resulting in the building of Thorns Primary School. As houses expanded into the area immediately surrounding Quarry Bank - as at Withymoor - further school building took place. Recent legislation that allows parents freedom of choice of schools for their children means that schools no longer think in terms of "catchment area" as they once did and the whole relationship between schools and the community in which they are located has become complicated.

The Mount Pleasant Local History Group has often discussed changes in the world of education especially as the group includes ex-pupils of all of Quarry Bank's schools. In 1998 the group produced a history of Mount Pleasant School to mark the school's 110th birthday in the present premises, and several members of the group have collected more information on education in Quarry Bank for this publication.

Below: Jack Williams supplied this picture of his class at Quarry Bank School in 1920. Jack is in the third row, 2nd from the right. He is standing between Jackie Jay and Edgar Cartwright, who later became the well-known organist at Cradley Forge chapel.

Left: The triumphant cricket team at Quarry bank School in the 1930s.
Standing left to right: Jack Cox, P.Doxey, Mr. Badger, Mr. Albert Tate, Mr. Cliff Wood, unknown and Raymond Raybould.
Bottom right: Felix Dunn, who later played for Worcester C.C.
(David Cox Collection)

Left: The triumphant football team 1925 -26 - winners of the Brierley Hill League.
The teachers in the back row are (left to right): Mr. Howard Aston, Mr. Albert Tate, Mr. Isaac Badger, the headmaster, and Billy Scriven.
(Phil Millward Collection)

Left: Children appearing in the "Pied Piper" at the Infants School in the mid 1960s. Robert (?) is palying his recorder as the Pied Piper, the others, left to right, are: Philip Smith, Judith Billingham and Richard Mason.
(Marie Billingham Colln.)

Thorns Primary School

Margaret Priest

To accommodate the growing population of Quarry Bank in the Caledonia Estate, the Thorns Primary school was built on land that had been donated for this purpose years earlier by John Stevens. It was land that had once been fields and open-cast mining - like so much of the land around Quarry Bank.

The official opening of the school was performed by Alderman William Harty at the beginning of the Easter Term in 1963. Miss Sturman was Headmistress, coming from the Girls Secondary School in Coppice Lane. When she retired Mr. David Howell was appointed.

One teacher who taught in the school from the day it opened until recently was Sue Homer, and this is what she recalls:

"I remember Thorns Road as a single carriageway, and much quieter. When the road works were in progress it caused a lot of disruption outside the school. One day there was great excitement when a stray horse wandered into the playground, and had to be lassoed with a skipping rope. At playtime it was quite a common occurrence for dogs to decide to join the children. It invariably created mayhem - screaming kiddies running round making the job of catching the runaway more difficult.

Thorns Primary has always been musically orientated, and the choir has performed at Dudley Town Hall, entertained elderly people in residential homes, and taken part in school concerts. The recorder groups have been popular and many pupils have had the advantage of learning to play a musical instrument.

Summer fayres have always done well, with fancy dress, lots of sideshows and refreshments and various attractions. One year we won first prize in the float competition in the Quarry Bank Gala. The saddest day was when Helen Reno, aged seven, was killed directly outside the school at lunchtime at a time before the road was made into a dual carriageway."

Since 1973 Barbara Smith has been a Dinner Lady and has seen many changes at the school. Barbara recalls:

"The little children used to sit at tables of eight and would be served by us. Grace was always said before the meal, and teachers sat with the little ones. The Juniors served themselves afterwards when tables had been wiped and cutlery set out. Crock plates and dishes were in use.

In the early days children were not allowed to bring sandwiches - it was school dinner or home to lunch. Roast dinners were on the menu every day, with fresh veg - all cooked on the premises. Chips were not available!

Over the years the system has been through a number of changes, and nowadays the whole meal is served on plastic trays. The little ones are still in first and are helped by us dinner ladies. Healthy eating is encouraged with a wide choice of food. Eg. roast meals, salads, quiches, chips, and various puddings. Some tables are set aside for "sandwiches" - a high proportion of the children preferring to bring their own lunch.

Today the children are much more confident, assertive, and noisier than they used to be although, mostly, they still remain "little darlings"."

Left: The cast of "Alladin" at Quarry Bank Infants School in 1959. Angela Ball, Susan Woodhouse, Shirley Hadlington, Glenys Ashman, Jennifer Hill, June Hill and Katheryn Southall.

(From the Collection of Shirley Winwood)

Mount Pleasant Primary School

On 10th September 1998 Mount Pleasant Primary School celebrated its 110th birthday. The aerial photograph printed here shows the school with the pupils lined up in the playground for the occasion - forming "1998".

The history of the school is told in the History Group's book "110 not Out", and readers should refer to that book to understand how the buildings have changed and expanded on this site. The first school at Mount Pleasant opened in 1882 in classrooms in the Sunday School building at the Wesleyan Chapel - on the site of the chapel's car park seen in the bottom right hand corner of this picture.

Right: Mount Pleasant infants in 1953. Left to right: Margaret ?, Clarice Guest, Ann ?, June Price, and Pauline Astley.
(Clarice Squires Collection)

Memories of Mount Pleasant

From Clarice Squires (nee Guest)

The recorder band was Mrs. Mantle's jewel, and I was proud to be part of it. I played descant and treble, but others also played tenor, some clarinets and flutes. We practised hard, sometimes during school hours, but always on Tuesday afternoons after school. Mrs. Mantle was a perfectionist and we would stay 'until we got it right'. "You are more trouble to me than money", she would say, but always with a smile and a twinkle in her eye.

Mrs. Mantle's Recorder Group at Kinver church, Christmas 1958. (Right to left) Dorothy Baker, Sylvia Holyoake, Clarice Guest, Maureen Plant, Susan Clark, Ann Campion, Susan Baker, Pauline Astley, Joyce Guise, Kathy Price, Janet Cartwright, June Price and Barbara Small.

Right: Miss Mantle's class at Kinver Church in 1956 - presenting a Christmas tableau. Keith Thomas, Margaret Sidaway (with lamb), Sheila Brookes, Barbara Small (shepherds), Ann Smith, Peter James (Joseph), Kathy Price (Mary), Sue Tunley (Angel), Alan James, Steven Dunn and Robert Lamb (Kings) and Joyce Guise. (Keith and Joyce sang.)

Both photographs come from the collection of Mrs. Mantle, who has celebrated her 100th birthday while this book was bring prepared. Additional information from Sue Smith (nee Tunley).

Her hard work with the recorder band certainly paid off. Not only did we tour the local factories and Darby & Joan at Christmas, but we regularly played at Kinver Christmas Church Carol Concert. Once we also went to a very posh garden party at Greenfields House in Stourbridge. Our greatest honour and joy to Mrs. Mantle was our being chosen, and actually winning the Music Festival at Moseley three years in a row.

My love of good music was born of her enthusiasm, and my life and education all the richer for good old Mount Pleasant.

Left: Mrs.Mantle established links between Mount Pleasant School and schools in America.
The main activity was the exchange of "pen-pal" letters.
Here we can see Mrs.Mantle's class opening presents that have just arrived from their American pen pals.
(Mrs. Mantle's Collection)

Carrying on the musical tradition at Quarry Bank Secondary School for Girls in Coppice Lane. The School Percussion Band in 1948.
(Betty Priest Collection)

The Girls' Secondary School had opened in 1932 at the same time as the Boys' School, but on the opposite side of Coppice Lane. Miss Woolridge had been headmistress from 1932 until 1951, followed by Miss Eccleston. From 1961 to 1961 the Headmistress was Miss Sturman who then went to Thorns Primary,

Left; Mr. Roberts with the Quarry Bank Secondary Boys School football team in 1950. Players include Ronnie Pritchard, Dicky Attwood, Brian Allport, Eddy Raybould, and Brian Wooldridge.
(Brian Wooldridg Colln.)

52

From Coppice Lane to the Thorns
Secondary Education in Quarry Bank

This topic was researched by **Bessie Cranton,** and expanded by **Margaret Priest** after consultation with Philip Millward, J. J. Martin and Simon Biggs.

Quarry Bank Secondary Boys School, in Coppice Lane, was opened in October 1932 with 287 on the roll, under the authority of the South West Staffordshire Divisional Executive. Alderman J. O. Whitehouse, Chairman of the Education Committee, officially opened the school in March 1933, along with the Girls Secondary School located on the opposite side of the road.

The school routine was interrupted on several occasions. For example, from 4th September to 26th September 1939 the schools were closed as a result of the National Emergency caused by the outbreak of the Second World War. They closed again on 8th and 9th May 1945 when a National Holiday was announced to mark the end of the War in Europe.

The mood of those years is captured by an entry in the school log for 31st October 1940: *"Girls were in the air-raid shelter from 1.45 until 3.35 pm when the alert sounded. They were then sent home since the shelters were wet and cold."*

During the second half of September each year the school closed when many of the pupils went hop-picking, although it is not clear when this practice ceased.

The Headmaster of the Boys' School was Mr. I. Badger until 1938 when Mr. W. Jeavons took over. Mr. Jeavons was a popular figure and it was during his time that the school was universally known by its nick-name: "Conk's College"! Mr. Jeavons remained Headmaster until May 1963 when Mr.J. J. Martin was appointed.

In 1966 Dudley County Borough assumed responsibility for the school, and in 1969 the Boys' School and the Girls' School merged to become Quarry Bank Secondary Mixed School, with 361 pupils on the roll. Miss Sturman, head of the Girls' School was appointed head of the newly opened Thorns Primary School, and Mr. Martin assumed responsibility for the amalgamated schools in Coppice Lane. The new intake was co-educational, as was the fifth year, but the years in between continued to be taught separately until those pupils had passed through the system.

The site of Thorns Community College, previously open-cast coal and clay mines, plus land belonging to Mousehall Farm, had already been earmarked for a new school. First of all, Murphys agreed to extract 5000 tons of coal and level the land, prior to the building programme commencing. In September 1973, at the completion of Phase 1 of the programme - "The Annex" - the first students moved onto the Thorns site.

The exodus from Coppice Lane was escalated when fire extensively damaged the former Boys' School building on 6th June 1974. The following year Thorns School was established as a Comprehensive School operating on the two sites. The difficulties of working out a timetable for a school on two sites was complicated in 1977 when a second fire destroyed much of the former Boys' School. The Main block had by then been completed at Stockwell Road, but to accommodate everybody on site the school had to use ten mobile classrooms as well as the Annex.

By 1980 the political climate had changed and funding for schools was different when Mr. F. Marshall took over the Headship in 1981. The concept of "community schools and colleges" was beginning to change the educational system - implying a much greater use of the school's facilities by all members of the community. A Sports, Leisure & Arts Block was built and in 1983 Thorns attained "Community College" status. The students now numbered 999.

A youth club was opened as the first community project, and a Senior Citizens Club was opened - which is still going strong after 17 years. The site was a "dual use" centre run jointly by the Education Department and Leisure Services. As might be expected, there were teething troubles in such a venture and a turbulent period followed as the school expanded in this dual role.

Mr.Marshall left in 1985 due to ill health, and for a time Ian Cleland was Acting Head, followed by Pat Wakefield. And then John Thompson, coming initially from Pensnett for just a term, was appointed Head. John Thompson's dream of a unified management of the school was finally realised in 1996. Meanwhile, there have been many extensions, opening of the Science & Mathematics Block in 1986, and in 1991 the Phase 5 Extension for English, Modern Languages and the new Reception Area.

In 1998 the new Post 16 Centre opened in conjunction with Stourbridge College, and the school today contains a vast range of facilities: alongside day to day school activities you can find a leisure centre, bar, adult education centre, letting facilities, and a network of contacts with the local community. Simon Biggs, as the Community Manager, has the arduous task of pulling all these strands together. Simon left Thorns on secondment to go to Warwick University to do an Advanced Diploma in Community Education, followed by a Masters Degree - so he is well qualified for the job.

Sylvia Tibbetts attended Quarry Bank Secondary School for Girls in 1951, when Miss Eccleston was Headmistress. Sylvia recalls:

I remember my first day at the school - after returning from hop-picking. I was proud of my new uniform: a brown tunic and cardigan, tie and beret, with a white blouse. After the first assembly I was told the hop-pickers were to remain behind to be directed into the classes - as the other pupils had commenced three weeks earlier.

There was a hockey pitch outside the building and netball courts in the playground. We also learnt that we were going to do cookery and gardening. My teacher was Mrs. Allen.

Although I was staying at school for dinner, I went home to fetch my PE kit. On returning, Miss Eccleston saw me pass the office window. She called me into her room and I expected a good telling off. She told me in a nice way that she was responsible for my welfare at dinnertime and not to do it again. I leant how to sneak through a window whenever I had to go home to fetch my PE kit after that!

Although I enjoyed every minute of attending Coppice Lane School, my time there was short-lived. I was taken into hospital. My friends in class each sent me a letter - but I was never to attend school again - owing to illness.

Staff at Quarry Bank Secondary School for Boys in 1964:
Roy Dernick, Geoff Attwood, Phil Millward, Al Warner, and Pete Shread. Front row: Jim Oakley Basil Hodgkinson, Jeff Martin (Headmaster), Jack Sidaway and Tony Brake.
(Phil Millward Collection)

Left: Phil Millward (right) and the school football team about 1964. Back row: John Sutton, Leon Oliver, ?, Michael Pearson, Michael Palmer, Alan Perks, John Cartwright.
Front row: Robert Glaze, Michael Quigley, Robert Little, Billy Welch, Michael Paget.
(Phil Millward Collection)

The above picture of class 2a at the Boys School in 1955 with their teacher, Harry Cox, also shows the view from the playground back towards the top of Quarry Bank High Street and the Oak Street area. Back row includes: Robert Cox, Michael Potts, Brian Clews, Ernie Clayton and Michael Pearson.

Middle row: Mr.Cox, Paul Sidaway, ?, Clive Johnson, Brian Partridge, Ernie Ketley, Alan Jones, Kenny Hill, Alan Southall, Paul Whiley, Keith Bloomer, Paul Jones.

Front row includes: Tony Round, Tony Yardley, Alan Williams, Michael Worton, John Potter, John Watton, Billy Deely, Michael Barnsley,Kenny Barber and Arthur ?.

(Collection of John Watton)

Left: Top row: A. Frost, J. Grosvenor, R. Yardley, J. Dudley, ?, B. James, T. Petford. Middle: K. Shaw, D. Deeley, R. Smith, B. Westwood, D. Perry, A. Picken. Bottom: C. Heath, A Coley, B. Hodkinson, W. Jeavons (Headmaster), K. Werritt, K. Homer, & R. Raybould.

Left: The school on fire in 1974

55

Left: The opening of the Sheffield Street Community Centre - 10th May 1961.
Cllr. Sam Woodhouse, Mr. Woodward, representing the builders, and, with his back to us, Cllr. F.J. Bradley, Chairman of Brierley Hill UDC, who has just received a silver key as a memento of the occasion.

Left: A fencing class in progress at the Community Centre in 1971. Left to right: Jean Timmins, May Fowkes, ?, ?, Dawn Davies, ?, Lorraine Parkes, ?, Vera Trevis and Ann Rubery. The main instructor for this class was a Mr. Bird, and it was organised as part of the programme of the thriving Ladies Club.

(Joyce Parkes Collection)

Children "getting into the act" outside the Community Centre in 1993 - part of Sarah Vaughan's Dance Group: Emma, Faye Redding, Haley Brooks, Kayleigh Nichol, Rebecca Milsum, Zowie.
Front row: Adam Rowe, Kelly Rowe, Emily Rowe and Jason Rowe.

Chapter 10
Quarry Bank Community Centre And Sheffield Street

What happens in Quarry Bank today, happens in Brierley Hill tomorrow!

Researched by **Charmayne Redding,** who acknowledges the help of several Quarry Bankers: **Sybil & Tom Genner, Sandra Vaughan, Paula Hughes, Lorna Whiley, Joe Jones and Mandy Rowe.**

The 10th May 1961 was a very proud day for Quarry Bank when its purpose-built Community Centre opened in Sheffield Street. Brierley Hill UDC had been committed to providing proper community centres since the end of the war, but up until that time had only managed to do so by converting existing premises rather than building new ones. Centres had opened at Wall Heath, Hawbush and Kingswinford, and Quarry Bankers were perhaps beginning to feel overlooked when suddenly it was announced that Quarry Bank would have the very first brand new purpose built centre in the district!

At least two other sites for a community centre in Quarry Bank were considered before the decision was made to use the corner of Sheffield Street. One quickly rejected idea was to use a site in Woodland Crescent, and the other idea was to use the former Coronet Cinema in Lower High Street. The council had been loathe to give the cinema owner any chance of putting the building to other use and he was therefore keen for the Council to buy it from him. The cost of converting the cinema to a centre would have been prohibitive.

By the time work began on the building in Sheffield Street, work had also begun on a new centre at Brockmoor and replacements at Hawbush and Wall Heath, but Quarry Bank beat them to it. Staffordshire County Council also contributed to these ventures and provided £4,267 towards the cost at Quarry Bank, out of a total cost of £11,000. It was designed by BHUDC's own architect, and was built by Thomas Holloway Ltd., of Tipton.

The centre was officially opened by Councillor Bradley, Chairman of BHUDC, and supported by Councillor Sam Woodhouse, and was blessed by Quarry Bank's vicar, Rev. Larkin. The opening of the centre seemed to precede the existence of a Community Association to run it, but nevertheless such an association quickly came into being, chaired by Ewart Bloor, and with Mrs. J. Parkes as Secretary and Sybil Genner as Treasurer.

Very quickly the centre became well-used. A youth club was established on Monday nights, Ladies Keep Fit on Tuesdays and Sewing on Thursdays. A Darby & Joan Club was set up to meet on Wednesday afternoons, and there were olde tyme dances and whist drives. The Young Wives came on Thursdays and the Operatic Society rehearsed on Friday evenings. There was a Tufty Club for children on Saturday mornings, and a nursery playgroup meeting every morning.

Barry and Sandra Vaughan took over the Youth Club with such success that it became a problem that they could only open one night a week - because that was all that was available at the Centre. Local newspapers took up the story that Quarry Bank still lacked adequate youth club facilities.

Up until the 1980s the Community Centre held an annual "open evening" when all the centre's users would showcase their activities - songs from the Darby & Joan, Keep-Fit displays, demonstrations from the Youth Club's netball team, and disco-dancing by the Pathfinders... plus two hundred people packed into the hall to see it all happening. However, something had gone wrong by the early 1990s and over half the centre's users had stopped supporting it. The Association was running at a loss and the Council was threatening to terminate the lease.

The Community Centre has now survived more than three decades - making a significant contribution to keeping alive the community spirit of Quarry Bank. Survival is not easy and at one time closure seemed to threaten but it has stayed open by becoming more self-funding. This in turn may have led to a charging policy that has led more groups from outside the area to use the centre, rather than immediately local groups. However, activities ranging from tap dancing to the Darby & Joan Club still go on at the hall and monthly car boot sales help raise funds!

The 1990s have witnessed new approaches to providing a focus to the intangible business of "community spirit". Some see it linked to education, and places like the Thorns School now boast community activities, others see it linked to health. Once it was linked to religion - reminding us that the Church Hall, a few yards from the Community Centre, is now closed. As we enter the new Millennium, towns like Quarry Bank face a real challenge about how to preserve, further cultivate, and provide for, community activity.

Sheffield Street before the Community Centre

Sheffield Street is one of the well-known streets of "old Quarry Bank" - associated with chain making and nail making in small backyard workshops. It set off at right angles to the High Street and abruptly stopped at the boundary of the fields that extended south of Coppice Lane. (Many roads in Quarry Bank are, or have been, cul-de-sacs.) Early in this century council houses were built in this field - "The White City" - and Sheffield Street extended into Saltwells Road to provide access to the new estate. In post-war years Woodland Avenue was extended and now runs into Sheffield Street via the Birch Coppice - a modern pub built at the end of the thoroughfare of that name. The old houses on either side of Sheffield Street have been cleared and thus it is now very difficult to imagine this was once a cul-de-sac (or "pudding bag street") serving only the homes and workshops of Quarry Bank's chain-makers.

Many people associated Sheffield Street with the poverty and squalor that surrounded chain-making, and indeed, in the 1900s, Sheffield Street was the centre of an outbreak of typhoid. Sixteen people died in this outbreak.

Descending Quarry Bank's steep High Street, one passed a large tree before turning into Sheffield Street and that tree seemed to provide a symbolic divide between the upper and lower portions of Quarry Bank - both geographically and socially! But that does not mean that the people who lived in 'lower' Quarry Bank felt any the worse for it. Lorna Whiley can recall her parents moving into no. 57 Sheffield Street about 1947.

The houses were already regarded as "condemned" at the time but the years she spent there were happy ones. Houses had outside wash-houses, shared communal yards and had outside toilets that were shared by two or three families. Some families kept pigs and there were many fowl pens. Her house was owned by the Webbs and a Mr. Nunn came around each week to collect the 7/6d rent. Some land was owned by the Genners and the Attwood brothers owned some of the chain shops. Even when Sheffield Street was going to be "cleared", care had to be taken to make sure that the Attwoods still had access to their chain shops at the back of the Sheffield Inn.

The Sheffield Inn

The degree to which Sheffield Street was a fairly self-contained community is shown by the fact that it contained a shop, and its own pub: The Sheffield Inn. Before the War, the licensee was Jospeh Bunn, then Thomas Bunn, but when he died in 1944, the licence passed to his widow Sarah Ellen. She continued to run the Sheffield until it closed in December 1956.

In the 1930s the Sheffield Inn had its own Horticultural Society, which organised up to three shows a year and a Harvest Festival. In doing so it raised funds for Corbett Hospital.

Below left: Raymond Kings winning the Archie Billingham cup and the Mary Pargetter Bowl at the 1962 Show. Below right : Janet Bunn with the ball of silver paper collected by her mother at the Sheffield Inn.

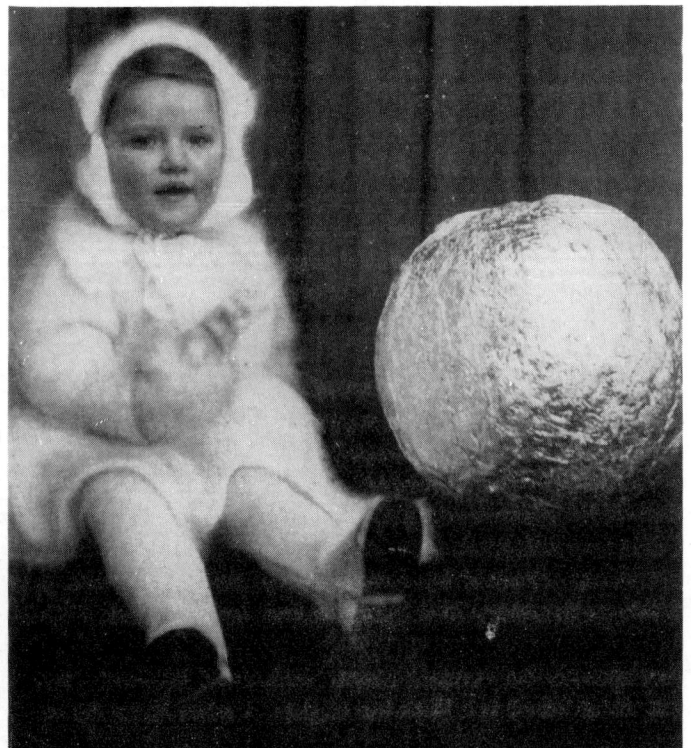

Right: The Sheffield Inn, Sheffield Street at the time when Jospeh Bunn was the licensee.

Looking from Birch Coppice back up towards Sheffieled Street today. Behind the shops to the right is Belle Vue which is still only accesible from Coppice Lane.

Sheffield Street

Sheffield Street: this map has been based on drawings submitted by Lorna Whiley and on several street maps of Quarry Bank. The buildings 59 to 64 Sheffield Street appear to form "Attwood's Row" with its surrounding chain shops. 14 -25 are the houses that many local people recall - standing well back from Sheffield Street, and with the row 26 -31 at right angles to the street. Opposite are the back to back houses and yards.

HIGH STREET.
57. LORNA WHILEY.
58. MRS. COOPER.
59. MRS. YARDLEY.
60. MRS. PRIEST.
61. MRS. GRAOTS.
62. MRS. LEWIS.
63. MRS. SMITH.

Left; Looking along School Passage today, one still looks towards the houses of the "White City" on the horizon. The school playground has been extended to the back of the houses in the extended part of Birch Coppice. This ground had once been the spoil heaps of Saltwells Colliery No. 33 pit. Bungalows now stand on the site of the houses marked 1 to 3 on the above map.

Chapter 11
Carnivals, Galas & Flower Shows

Based on the work of **Bessie Cranton** - with additional information supplied by **Don Manley, Brian Wooldridge, Shirley Winwood, John James** and others.

Introduction

By the time Quarry Bank had acquired the dignified status of being an "Urban District", towards the end of the nineteenth century, its population had grown and developed socially to the extent that the town supported numerous events which expressed what we would now call "community spirit". Such public occasions first took the form of processions to Sunday School picnics, and parades of Friendly Society members and their banners. Parades and community events were also organised to celebrate great occasions such as Coronations and Jubilees - the parades at the time of King George V's Coronation in 1911 being the subject of a number of photographs.

Between the wars there were galas which were run by the Hospital Committee - raising funds for the Corbett Hospital. The founder of the Hospital Committee was Artie Billingham, and the Secretary was C. Bird. Ernest Stevens was the President for a number of years. The Allotment Society also raised funds for the hospital by running the Flower & Vegetable Show at the Liberal Club.

After the Second World War the Quarry Bank Gala was revived, by the British Legion in order to raise funds for the Brighter Old Age Committee, and the Flower & Vegetable Shows were held alongside the Gala in Stevens Park.

The Galas organised to raise funds for the Brighter Old Age Committee ceased in 1973 and there was a gap before the gala was revived in 1988 to raise funds for Cancer Research. Thus, there are really three distinct periods of "gala history" - the pre-war galas, followed by two periods of post-war gala.

Right: Parades and processions always seem to have been very popular in Quarry Bank.
Children fill the High Street as far as they eye can see in the parade organised to celebrate the Coronation of King George V in June 1911. Like all parades that took place before the opening of Stevens Park in 1921, this one lacked an obvious destination. Fields were usually used to hold picnics at the end of such events.

(Margaret Yates Collection)

Right: After the opening of Stevens Park, parades could be organised that terminated in the park. The Hospital Fetes and adjoining Horticultural Shows then became popular annual events. About 1930 we see the Labour Club "float" on a dray in Thorns Road. The club won first prize for this "Rock of Ages" tableaux featuring (Left to right) Beryl Maybury, Joan Guest, unknown, Elsie Homer, Edith Guest and Elsie Griffiths.

(Elsie Payne Collection)

61

Carnivals and Galas

Left: Jack and Madge Williams outside their mother's shop in High Street Quarry Bank watching a late 1920s or early 1930s carnival procession. Their mother had made them paper costumes to wear for the occasion but regarded them as too young to join the procession.

(Madge Richards' Collection)

Above: The Gala Queen's crown and the tiaras of her attendants (Princesses?), used in the first phase of the post-war galas. (Now carefully preserved!)

Bottom Left: A late 1950s Gala Queen stands on the steps of the bandstand in Stevens Park.

Bottom Right: Eileen Hadlington in 1951 "Festival of Britain" costume in one of the Fancy Dress Competitions. Eileen became Gala Queen in 1961.

(Eileen Thompson's Collection)

Ox roasts, Fancy Dress & Gala Queens:

Right: The World's Champion Ox-roaster - Harry Johnson - had to come all the way from Cradley Heath to attend the 1957 Gala and sets to work in Stevens Park.

Right: Judges and guests plus entrants in the childrens' Fancy Dress Competition line up on the tennis courts at the 1955 Gala. On the left are Stan and Jean Hill, Stan being Chairman of Brierley Hill UDC. Next to them is John Talbot MP, and Ewart Bloor stands by the "lighthouse".

Right: John Talbot MP crowns Doreen Wooldridge as Gala Queen in 1958. On the left are Mr. Wyatt and Angela Bridgwater, on the right is Merle Willetts.
(Brian Wooldridge Collection)

The Post-War Galas

Some kind of gala was held in 1951 to mark "The Festival of Britain", but the first of the post-war "galas" appears to have been held in 1952. A year later the activities took on an added significance in celebrating the Coronation of Elizabeth II. As the 1950s went on the gala developed and became an important part of the Quarry Bank social calendar.

A report of the 1958 Gala tells us:

"Nearly 13,000 attended the Gala in Stevens Park in brilliant sunshine, raising about £600 for the Brighter Old Age Fund.

The gala included a flower show, police dog display, Civil Defence demonstration, archery display, variety show and women's football - followed by dancing on the tennis courts in the evening. The Welfare Section of the Brierley Hill Civil Defence Team served food continuously for six and a half hours - and sold 2 cwt of sausages in 2,668 hot dogs! Mr. Leslie White walked round the park in old English Gentleman's attire carrying a ham - and raised £50 by doing so!"

By the 1960s the Gala was being ably organised by a committee chaired by Horace Hadley, who ran a cooked meats shop in New Street, with Bill Henley as the Secretary. Both men were local councillors. Mr. Grove, the butcher at 56 High Street, was the Treasurer. Mrs. Fletcher, who was also the President of the Brighter Old Age Committee, was President of the Gala Committee.

Don Manley came to live in Quarry Bank in 1959 when he started teaching at Coppice Lane. One night he met Bill Henly in a pub and Bill invited him to join in the work of organising the Gala. Soon Don was organising the Flower Show. Later he became treasurer and then organiser and chairman. Looking through old Gala programmes it is possible to pick out other well-known local names who played their part in running the galas - for example William Hanke was stewarding the flower show in 1962.

During the early years of the Gala the activities began a week before Gala Day - usually starting with a Blessing Service held in the Parish Church, followed by dances, whist drives, baby shows and, later, bingo sessions. On the big day itself it was important to select a suitable attraction to head the procession, so for example, in 1961, it was led by the Dagenham Girl Pipers. The procession itself would consist of numerous floats representing local organisations and groups.

To attract as many people as possible to watch the procession and to come to the Gala activities in Stevens Park it became more and more important to find the right person to open the proceedings. Obviously it had to be someone with "star" quality but one that would not charge the Committee so much that the funds would be seriously depleted. In 1961 and 1962 the committee got away with using local dignitaries - local MPs, figures from Brierley Hill Council etc, but by 1963 these figures were still invited but had to take a back seat to someone more likely to draw the crowds.

On 31st August 1963 Elsie Tanner (Pat Phoenix) swept into Quarry Bank from Coronation Street - bringing plenty of rain with her. The appalling weather produced three good outcomes - Pat offered to come back the following year without charging her usual fee of £90, the Committee collected a £400 payment from an insurance company because Don Manley had persuaded them to insure against bad weather, and many supporters felt the effects of the "wash-out" could best be reversed by taking the collecting tins round the pubs that night - with record results!

Pat Phoenix did return in 1964 but the following year something a little different was tried by having the gala opened by Johnny Prescott - a British Heavy-weight boxing champion. Local muscle was provided by John Talbot MP, Miss Pearson who was Chairman of BHUDC and Kate Rogers in her capacity as a County Councillor!

Coronation Street provided someone to open 1967's Gala - this time in the shape of Len Fairclough (Peter Adamson), and ATV's Jean Morton came along in 1968. Perhaps it was inevitable that the job was given back to a local dignitary in 1969 as the Mayor of Dudley - who performed the opening - was none other than Councillor Bill Henley, who had contributed much to the work of the Gala Committee over the years.

The huge crowds associated with the post-war galas turned out in the early 1970s to see the likes of Diana Dors (1972) and Barbara Windsor (1973) come to Stevens Park. This called upon Don Manley's showmanship skills and when asked about this early in 1999, he recalled:

"One problem was to make sure the celebrity made a surprise entry to the park without being spotted too soon. This was quite difficult in the case of Diana Dors who arrived conspicuously in a large white chauffeur driven Rolls Royce. Don arranged for such stars to arrive at his house in Acres Road, where they could change and then make a dash for the park across Thorns Road. Barbara Windsor arrived in the same way.

Perhaps the best publicity the gala ever received was during the year (1969) when the gala committee advertised for Lady Godivas. They ended up with ten hopeful Lady Godivas, but only three horses - which meant choosing only the best Lady Godivas or persuading the others to appear on bikes!"

The local newspaper report of the 1972 event records the scale of the gala's success:

The 1961 Gala:

In 1961 local councillors were still formally opening the Gala - soon (in 1963) to be replaced by "celebrities", but this was the year that the Dagenham Girl Pipers led the procession.

Right: Councillor Homer opens the gala from a platform built in front of the old pavilion in Stevens Park. Behind is the Gala Queen, Eileen Hadlington and her two princesses - Pat Cox and Maureen Hill.

Right: Gala Queen Eileen Hadlington, an eighteen year old hairdresser, is helped down from the platform after the opening ceremony in 1961. Horace Hadley on the left, Councillor Bill Henley on the right - both members of the Gala Committee. The good weather and success of the 1961 gala made up for the rain and misery of 1960.
(Both pictures from Eileen Thompson's Collection.)

Left: Gala Queen, Eileen Hadlington, presents the Rose Bowl to the flower show "champion" in 1961. The bowl was donated by Mrs. F.A. Light to the Brighter Old Age Committee, and is still to be found in Quarry Bank.

(All photos on this page from the collection of Eileen Thompson)

"Saturday's Quarry Bank Gala must go down as the most successful to date, with a number of new records established, not least of which was that 10,000 people paid to get in to the fun on Stevens Park.

Gate receipts were consequently higher and the Gala Committee are hoping that for the fourth successive year profits will top the £1000 mark for the benefit of the Quarry Bank Brighter Old Age Fund, which last year gave £2600 to local old folk.

The weather was generally disappointing - cloudy and cool - but the large crowds seemed hardly to notice it as they awaited the arrival of film and television star Diana Dors to open the Gala.

Immediately after the opening ceremony, which was also attended by Brierley Hill MP., Fergus Montgomery, and Mrs. Montgomery, and the Mayor and Mayoress of Dudley, Alderman and Mrs. E Morris, Diana Dors was one of three judges for a "Miss Industry" competition involving some of the prettiest girls in local commerce and industry.

The unanimous choice was Mrs. June Greenham, "Miss Titford Motor Services", who lives in Lower Gornal.

The Mayor and Mayoress also judged the best fancy dress, and Mr. Harry Whale was judge at the flower and vegetable show. At the latter, the Silver Championship Cup for the entrant to win the most points was won by Mr. H. Elnor.

Attractions during the afternoon included a crisp eating competition, whippett racing, and the funfair. The demonstration by The Royal Artillery did not take place, nor did the mini circus."

This gives some idea of the number of activities that went on around the gala - from whippet racing to dancing on the tennis courts or at the Community Centre. Sporting events were often held alongside the gala. For example, in 1962 these included a football match between Quarry Bank Celtic v Stourbridge Reserves. In 1965 it was a match between Dunns Bank and Brierley Hill Youth Club. The same year there was a bowls match between members of the local Press v. Local Councillors!

Local names are encountered once again in 1969 when a grand raffle was organised - the first prize was one week's holiday for two people in Jersey - presented by Genners' Coaches and Hadley's Coaches - both well known Quarry Bank firms. The second prize was donated by British Rail & Pontins, but the third prize came from another Quarry Bank travel firm: Homer's Coaches offered a weekend for two in Blackpool. Tickets were 1/- each (5p).

The Gala presented for the benefit of the Brighter Old Age Committee had run successfully from 1952 through to 1973 but then abruptly ceased. There was a fourteen year gap before the carnival was revived yet again.

Left: Gala Programmes

Above: At one time the Gala Procession was often led by this "glamour girl" - local railwayman, Les Wyatt plus pram.

Right: The children of Coppice Close providing a float in the 1971 Gala.
(Brian Wooldridge Collection)

Right: The children of Coppice Close in fancy dress for the 1970 Gala. (Brian Wooldridge)

Right: Quarry Bank Gala 1967 and the Gala Queen and her attendants ride the procession on the back of one of Jack Genner's lorries.
(Collection of Pat Cox)

About the time that the "old" carnivals ceased, a group came into being with the intention of raising funds for Imperial Cancer Research. In August 1987 this group held a fund-raising "Fun Day" at Brockmoor Community Centre. The weather was good and the event was a great success. Two of the organisers were Shirley Winwood and Tracey McNulty. Inspired by success, Tracey set off to see Dudley Council about using Stevens Park - and thus they found themselves reviving the Quarry Bank Carnival in July 1988. It rained on Carnival Day in 1988 but the crowds supported it anyway and the event was back on the map. From the following year onwards other local charities began to benefit from the collections but Imperial Cancer Research remained the principal benefactor.

Shirley, Tracey, and their hard working group, mounted eleven carnivals - about half of which enjoyed the effects of good weather. Trying out dates in May or June did not manage to guarantee good weather! In 1998 the Carnival seemed to face a number of problems - in addition to the general trend towards less public interest in such events. Roadworks designed to improve access to Merry Hill forced the abandonment of the procession, and that led to the event having no "Queen". A rather modest event therefore opened in Stevens Park in relatively poor weather. The exhausted group of organisers felt carnivals have had their day in Quarry Bank - at least for the time being - but the group still continues to raise money for Cancer Research. A small scale Family Fun Day was held in June 1999 in the grounds of the Quarry Bank School organised by the Quarry Bank Arts, Education and Health Group.

Quarry Bank Galas - The Facts
Opened by:

1988	Cradley Heath Speedway Team
1989	Derek Dougan
1990	-
1991	Simon Cross (Speedway rider)
1992	Harry Harrison
1993	Tommy Mundon
1994	Nightshade and Shadow (of The Gladiators)
1995	Ainsley Harriott
1996	John Odell impersonating Alf Garnet
1997	Barrell House Blues Band
1998	Sonya Siviter (97 Gala Queen)

Recent Gala Queens at a Glance
1988	Jeanne Frith
1989	Lisa Bissell
1990	Helen Totney
1991	Kelly Morris
1992	Donna James
1993	Gemma Hayward
1994	Sarah Southwick
1995	Emma Blakemore (Prince: Richard Leeson, Princess: Kelly Wyte)
1996	Debbie Coley (Prince: Jason Oakley, Princess: Kaylee Asbury)
1997	Sonya Siviter (Princess: Lindsey Dewfield)
1998	No Gala Queen

In the early 1950s the fairground amusements were apparently provided by Ernie Steel, but later by Henry Harvey. In more recent times the fair has been provided by the Jones family from their base in Cradley Heath, or by Wilsons of Redditch acting on their behalf.

The 1990 Gala Procession passes along the High Street.
(Shirley Winwood)

The June 1990 Gala:

Right: Young Quarry Bankers appear as Red Indians on one of the floats. (Shirley Winwood)

Right: Helen Totney - the 1990 Gala Queen (centre) with her attendants, Karen Yates and Donna Joynes.

The Flower Show at the Labour Club - 18th September 1971.

Left to right: George Collett, the Show Secretary, Anne Reynolds, the cake judge, and Gerald Dunn, steward.

Flower & Vegetable Shows

The Flower & Vegetable shows prospered in the big marquee in Stevens Park and competition for the various trophies was strong. One such trophy was the cut glass bowl presented by Councillor Mary Pargetter - awarded to the exhibitor gaining the most points over-all. The Artie Billingham Memorial Cup was awarded to the exhibitor gaining the most points in the vegetable classes, and the Rose Bowl presented by Mrs. Annie Light went to the exhibitor gaining most points in the flower classes.

The Silver Championship Cup was presented by Mr. Dennis A Wood to the winner of a competition organised between pubs for collective display of flowers, fruit and vegetables.

Other Horticultural Activities

The Flower and Vegetable Show held alongside the Gala was not the sum total of Quarry Bank's horticultural history. A Horticultural Show was also started at the Labour Club about 1965 with many classes to enter - including classes for making cakes! A Stan Millward Memorial Vase was awarded to the best exhibit in the show. The Mitchell & Butler Shield went to the exhibitor with the most points, and there was also a Society Vase.

About the same time an Early Chrysanthemum show was initiated at the Community Centre and a cut glass vase, donated by William Hanke, was presented to the winning exhibitor. Other Quarry Bankers took a great interest in the cultivation of roses - Messrs Cranton, Hill and Siviter helped organise the Midland Rose Society and its shows. All these events brought Quarry Bankers with horticultural interests together socially.

More recently Dunns Bank rose grower Ernest Hill bred a new vermilion red rose called "Royal Visit". This rose was named to mark Queen Elizabeth II's visit to Dudley in June 1994.

Left: The Artie Billingham Cup, presented by the pre-war Hospital Carnival Committee in memory of his thirty year's service to the cause, and the Horticultural Trophy. The Rose Bowl Trophy and, below, the 1972 Horticultural Show programme

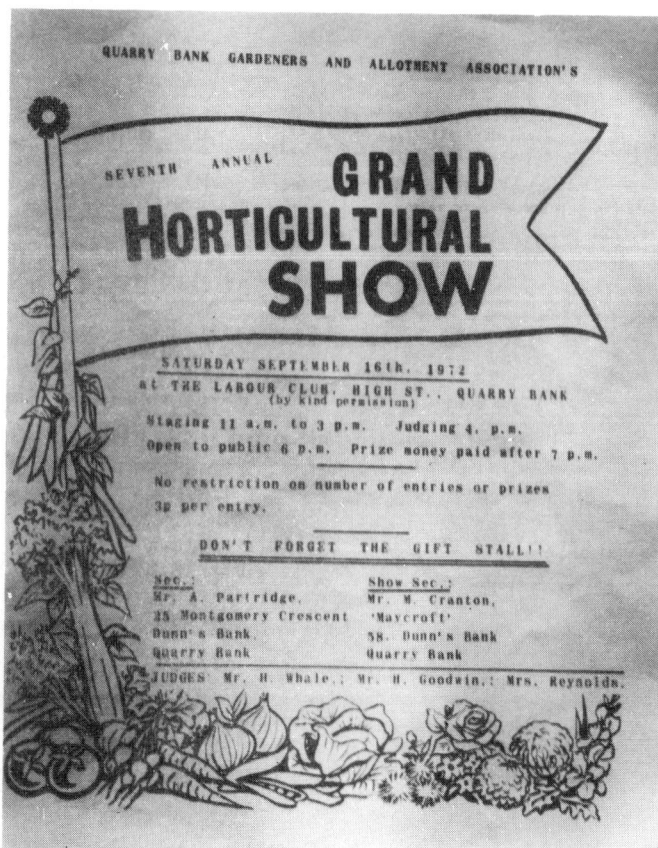

Chapter 12
Leisure in Quarry Bank

1. Social Events

In the previous chapter we noted the popularity of parades and galas in Quarry Bank.

Right: Quarry Bankers, in the Maughan Street area celebrate the Coronation of Queen Elizabeth II with a street party and crown-shaped cake on 2nd June 1953. The cake was made by Mrs. Reynolds, who supplied the photograph.

Right: the Jubilee Party held in 1977 was held on the school playing field, Coppice Lane. Phylis Price shows off contestants in a nobbly knee contest.
Dr. Fair and her husband Major are the couple seen on the bench on the left.
(Phylis Price Collection)

Right: Solid-tyred "charas" line up in the High Street, between Oak Street and Sun Street in the early 1920s for a works outing. The coach in the foreground is a Burford 20-seater licensed to Sammy Johnson's Coach Company in May 1920.

2. Entertainment

Quarry Bank may have never had an Opera House but it seems to have its fair share of entertainment.

The Coronet Cinema was a much loved institution from 1933 to 1960, and live entertainment on stage was provided on an amateur basis by the companies that grew out of the Musical Society established at Cradley Forge Church.

In the early years of this century Pat Collins brought fairground entertainment to the Quarry Bank Wake held on ground at the back of the Royal Oak at the junction of High Street and Oak Street.

In the 1920s Bailey's Circus spent some time on this site. In more recent times, the park has been host to the fairs, to accompany the gala on the November bonfires. The circus has also occasionally come to Stevens Park.

Above: The Coronet Cinema decorated for the Coronation in 1953.
Harold Roberts - manager and part-owner of the Coronet.
(Celia Thorneycroft Colln.)

Cradley Forge Amateur & Dramatic Society Productions. Left to right: Joan Thomas, Jack Felton, Ernie Webb, Dick Bedford, and Maud Felton.

Dick Bedford and Ernie Webb are hidden beneath wigs in the centre of the first and second rows.
Standing at the back: Horace and Norman Bucknall, responsible for lighting and production.

(Vera Dunn Collection)

Above: Quarry Bank Conservative Club outing to the Houses of Parliament.
(Mary Brookes)

Left: Another operatic production at Cradley Forge.
(Brenda Holloway)

Left: Quarry Bank Scouts in the 1930s. Harry Hawkeswood, the Scout Master is in the middle of the back row.
(Sue Smith's Colln.)

3. The Scouts

Notes by **Jack Beddall**

The Scouts Association Registration Forms show that Quarry Bank 1st Scouts were formed in 1922, and were controlled by the Parish Church. The headquarters were in the Church Sunday School building in Victoria Road, and the Scout Master was F.N. Pardoe. Fifty three scouts joined the troop.

In 1928 the Scouts moved from Victoria Road to the new headquarters in Maughan Street. The Scout Master was then Harry Hawkeswood and the Cub Master was E. Billingham.

In 1972 the Maughan Street hut was burnt down - owing to its age. The Scouts then moved to West Street for a time. Meanwhile Dudley Council gave them two new huts, which were erected in Bobs Coppice Walk about 1978. The huts were set on fire and a new replacement building in brick was opened on 13th December 1980. This is the building that stands on the site today.

In 1981 the Lye Primitive Methodist Scouts joined the Quarry Bank Scouts as "Sea Scouts", but in 1986 they changed back to the "1st Quarry Bank Scouts". The present Group Scout Leader is Trevor Pearson, the Scout Leader is Tim Scott, the Cub Scout Leader is Fran Sedgley and Stuart Harrison is Honorary Scouter.

Ten Beavers, twenty Cubs, four Scouts and three Venture Scouts make up the Scout Troop today.

Quarry Bank Scouts out at the Camp established at Kinver. Cyril Coulter, who joined in 1922, recalls that the Quarry Bank troop spent a lot of time building this camp, which has since been used by Scouts from all over the area.

Taking a rest during the work on building the brick-built Scout HQ at Bobs Coppice Walk in 1980. Michael Holloway and Bob Hadley take tea supplied by the group's committee members.

(NB - Scout photographs appear in Quarry Bank in old Photographs - pages 104/105.

Chapter 13
Sport in Quarry Bank

In Quarry Bank in Old Photographs we presented pictures that showed the variety of sporting activity that has gone on in Quarry Bank - from Football to Badminton, from Cricket and Tennis to Dog Breeding and Bowls! This time round we concentrate on Football.

Boys who had played football at school, or had kicked a rag-covered brick around the yard, were encouraged to play for the "Old Boys" teams that were started. Here we see the Mount Pleasant Old Boys of 1928/29.
Back row: Vic Palmer,?, Thompson, ?, Webb,?.
Middle: ?, Harcourt Wooton, Clover, Fred Roberts, Alf Palmer.
Front: ?, Fornham Batham, Bill Brown.

Other teams grew up around pubs, chapels etc.
Below: Saltwells F.C. of 1938/39. Unfortunately no one has been identified apart from Albert Guest, of Sheffield Street, on the extreme right.

Quarry Bank Celtic Football Club

The story of Quarry Bank Celtic Football Club goes back to a legendary club that used that name from about 1912 to 1919. Very little is now known about that club except that it was based at The Vine Inn in the High Street and that the team had to walk from there to a pitch that was in the area now occupied by Westfield Road. It is assumed that the club found it increasingly difficult to find young players as the First World war progressed and thus it faded away. The Vine was the headquarters of various sporting organisations in Quarry Bank - including pigeon flying - but the pub has also vanished into history as the building is now occupied by dental technicians.

Between the wars Quarry Bank did not seem to lack football teams as there were Chapel-based teams, works teams and teams of "old boys" from the schools, but there did not seem to be one team that could claim to represent the whole community. This gap was to be filled by the emergence of a new Quarry Bank Celtic.

Cyril Cartwright tells the story:

I was born in Bower Lane, Quarry Bank, and went to the Coppice Lane School.

My life has been involved with the Celtic since 1944, and I have been Secretary of the club since 1945. We started in 1944 as a group of lads just leaving school. We were a group of pals who had all been to the Coppice Lane School, and had knocked about together. The War was on by then and there didn't seem a lot for lads to do in those days - so we played football whenever we could - with anything that could be used as a ball. We would play in the park most evenings until it was dark, and were always talking about setting up a proper team. At the time there was a team at the Jury, there was Quarry Bank Rangers and the Quarry Bank Juniors - but I think The Juniors finished at about the time we were thinking of setting up.

When we actually organised ourselves as a team we registered with the Birmingham County FA as Quarry Bank Celtic but on the registration cards of the Halesowen Youth League we had called ourselves Quarry Bank Juniors so we had to make up our minds once for all what we wanted to call ourselves. Mr. and Mrs. Kendall took an early interest in our club. They were in business next door to the Vine with a general furniture store and the wine shop next door, and Mr. Kendall told us there had once been a team called the Celtic but there was no real connection between our club and the former one.

We went into the Halesowen Youth League and played in the Stevens Park in Quarry Bank - on the small ground. Immediately we started it looked as if the club migh founder as lads were called up to go into the Services. Another founder member - Bill Hamblett - suggested that I took on the Secretary's job as he reckoned I was good at writing. Whether I was good at it or not, I have certainly had enough practice ever since!

The first balance sheet I saw at our first AGM showed we had a surplus of 2/9d which wouldn't take us very far. We hadn't set the Halesowen Youth League on fire, and out future seemed uncertain but I felt determined to somehow make a go of it.

Having taken on the job of Secretary, I found myself taking on the job of Manager as well from October 1945 onwards. At that time we went into the Brierley Hill Amateur Football League, Second Division. We lost one league match during that first 1945/46 season - we won almost everything that came along. Faced with success I decided we needed to take players from further afield, although there was some opposition from lads who thought we should keep to just Quarry Bank players. Obviously there has always been a nucleus of Quarry Bank players but I went around and brought players in from all over the place - to maintain our status as a successful team.

In the second year that I was Secretary/Manager we developed a Reserve Team, and by 1947 we were able to run three teams. On Christmas Day 1947 Quarry Bank Celtic fielded three teams - kicking off at eleven o'clock on Christmas morning. The First team played in the park - easily winning with ten goals. The Reserves played the A Team who were in the third division of the Brierley Hill League. The Reserves won the match: 4:2. We are the only club in Quarry Bank which has run three teams, and we were the first junior side to play with numbers on. I had less trouble then running three teams than I now have in running one! We had no cars or telephones yet we managed to run three teams. We were also the only football club in Quarry Bank to play in semi-professional matches.

As time went on we had badges put on the shirts, and we are one of the few clubs around today who play with our badges on. The badge includes the Scottish thistle and the Staffordshire knot - because Quarry Bank was in Staffordshire then. We've always like to turn out as smart team. I think I chose the colours because I'd always had a bit of a leaning towards the Albion, although in the club we were fairly evenly divided between those who favoured The Wolves, and those who favoured Albion or The Villa. We didn't play in stripes for three or four seasons although Mr. Kendall told us the original Celtic had played in stripes. You couldn't get striped shirts in wartime so we had to make do.

During the War you had to collect coupons to be able to buy strip. During the season before I became Secretary, the team had played in red and white stripes simply because we had been able to buy a few second hand shirts from the Saltwells team. The first new strip that we bought was blue shirts with white collars and they cost us £5/14/6d - which was a lot of money at the time. We had blue stockings and white shorts that were made out of flour sacks. I bought these Canadian flour sacks and boiled them until all trace of any print or colour was washed out of them. I found a lady who was good at making up things and she made them into shorts.

Later I bought a set of white hospital shirts from a shop in the arcade at Stourbridge. They were surplus stock from Corbett Hospital and we then played in blue shorts, blue stockings and white shirts with our badges sewn on them. Three years later I sold the white shirts - minus the badges - and made a profit on them! Although strip was cheaper in those days than it is now, you have to remember that lads weren't earning very much and were then paying between 1/- and 1/3d club money. Players had to buy their own boots.

When in the Second Division of the Brierley Hill League, we won the Malin Cup. We were losing 2-0 at half time, against Halesowen Youth Club, and Les Smith was playing against us who later played for Wolves and for England. However by the end of the match we had won 3:2. It was a great moment, but that was actually the second trophy that we won. The first trophy we won was the Brierley Hill Second Division League Cup when we beat Wall Heath Boys Club at Stuarts' ground. The previous week we had lost to them on the same ground: 3:0 - in the semi-final of the Albion Shield. We travelled to the match in one of Genner's coaches and came back with the League Cup having won 3:0. I was over the moon.

We stayed in the Second Division for a second year before being promoted, and during that second year we became the first Second Division team to win the Corbett Hospital Trophy. We played against Miners

Welfare on Lye Town's ground and we were losing the game 2:1 with only a few minutes to go - then we equalised with a disputed penalty and then we won 5:2 in the extra time! We won the same cup again the next year when we beat the Two Gates team, 5:4. They were a mighty side who had been playing for years. It was a smashing game played on Stourbridge Town's ground.

We went into the First Division but weren't too pleased with the way things turned out. We were hoping to be runners-up in that division but we played against Woodside in Holly Hall Park and they were short of a player. We lent them one of our players and he scored a couple goals that enabled them to beat us! Having ended up third in that league we decided to try the Handsworth League in 1948.

We won the Handsworth League in our first season with them, but it was a very tough league. We only stayed in that league for the one season and then went into the Birmingham Alliance and finished as runners-up. Even so we had a smashing evening game in which we beat the champions 6:0 in the final of the Cadbury Cup, but that began a period when we began to lose players to other clubs. We lost at least five players who went to plays for teams in the Birmingham League - joining semi-professional teams like Stourbridge, Cradley Heath, Brierley Hill Alliance, or Lye Town.

We stayed in the Birmingham Alliance for about three years but I feel that we lost our way for a time. We applied to join the Worcestershire Combination (now known as the Midlands Combination), were turned down a few times, but finally joined in 1953. It was one of the happiest moments in my life when I went along to the Gate Hangs Well - where our club met - to be able to tell the lads that we had been admitted at last to the Combination.

We stayed in the Combination for nineteen years. We were eventually relegated to the Second Division -

Right: Quarry Bank Celtic F. C. 1945/46, taken in a studio at Halesowen, wearing shorts made from sacks! Standing: W. Hamblett, R. Checketts, C. Cooper, E. Evans, B. Stevens, S. Bloomer, C.M. Cartwright(Secretary/Manager). Seated: R.Waldron, R. Jasper, F. Knight, N. Allen, T. Cartwright. Front Row: V. Clemeents, & C.Cannop.
Trophies: Brierley Hill 2nd Div. League Cup and the Malin Trophy.

ironically a division that I had suggested creating as way of helping clubs keep their reserve players. One factor that dragged against us during all those years was that we played on Stevens Park where the facilities weren't that good. It wasn't a proper enclosed ground and we were playing against the reserves of clubs that had their own grounds. I think our failure to be re-elected to the First Division in the Combination was one of the biggest disappointments in my life, but during our time we had played in six finals, had won the Dudley Guest Hospital cup twice, and during our best season had been sixth in the Combination.

The Council did build some new dressing rooms in Stevens Park but they were built to fit in with the rest of the scenery at the park rather than to a practical design. Our first game we played in the Combination was against Stourbridge Reserves at home in Stevens Park. I had five hundred programmes printed and we sold out. We must have had about a thousand spectators standing all the way round our pitch and we drew 2:2 which was a creditable performance. But the irony was we couldn't charge anyone to watch the match because it was simply public space in the park. The only way we could try and generate income for the club was to sell raffle tickets at sixpence a time.

I did go after a couple of grounds over the years, without success. One ground I would have liked was a sports field used by The Jury. I went to see one of the directors of the Jury but he told me that a school was going to built on the ground. We thought we were being fobbed off - but, sure enough, years later the Thorns School was built there!

The club has never been in any trouble financially and we've never owed anybody any money. We've always been very respected and we've stuck to the rules, so you can imagine that it was upsetting to come out of the Combination in 1972. We then went into the Wolverhampton Amateur League for three years in which we lost more players. We also kept a reserve team in the Brierley Hill League Second Division as we were down to two teams by then. They were promoted 1981/82 to the First Division in what was by then known as the Dudley Metro Combination. We stayed in there until 1989/90 when that league competition folded up.

Our worst time was in 1975 when we went to having just the one team - but we survived and when the Dudley Metro packed up we took our team into the Kidderminster League - and we are still in there now. We went to the semi-final of their Junior Cup this season.

Nowadays the committee meets once a month at the Dock & Iron in Delph Road (formerly the Duke William), but I can remember the days when the club met every week at The Gate Hangs Well and the room would be packed with thirty or so chaps. Today it is difficult to find chaps who want to take part in running the club, but over the years I have done all sorts of things to keep things going - I've run the line (not something that's a good idea when you are in your seventies!), I've refereed, I've put the ropes round the ground, I've put the nets up, I've marked the ground out, I've put refreshments on, I've washed the kit, and I've driven the coach to the away matches. (Homer's used to provide us with a coach and I had a PSV licence because I've always been interested in driving.) I've also played for Celtic - but only when we were desperate for players.

We had many outstanding players over the years so in a way it's not fair to name a few and ignore the others, but one or two ought to be named. One chap is still on our committee now - Colin Connop - he was a marvellous player. He's not a very big chap but he played centre forward and during the first season he played for us he scored seventy four goals - nine of which were in one match! Sid Ashmore was another centre forward who married a Quarry Bank girl and came along to play for us - I should think that he and Colin scored over three hundred goals each for Celtic over the years. In February 1951 we were playing Northfield Town and we were losing 6:0 not long before half time - but then Sid scored a goal. In the end we won 7:6 and Sid had scored six of our goals! Another skilful player I will never forget is Dennis Stanworth - he played what was known then as a wing half - he captained each of our three teams in his time. Another centre forward of note was Ray Kettle, ex Stourbridge F.C., who saved over 100 goals in the Combination for Celtic.

We didn't have many players who went on to play for professional sides - but Trevor Hadley went on to play for Albion's Wednesday League side but broke his leg while playing for us and therefore did not go on to greater things. Stanley Dunn was a Quarry Banker who played for us and went on to semi-professional sides. Two full backs played for us for a long while - Bert Yardley and the late Eric Neale who later became Chairman of the club. A goal-keeper worth remembering was Colin Homer. Bill Hamblett, one of the founder members and now President of our club was another brilliant player - he later played for Brierley Hill and Stourbridge.

As a rough guess, I would think that about seven hundred chaps have played for Celtic over the years, some staying for as long as fourteen years. We have one chap playing for us at the moment - Paul Collins - who has been playing for Celtic for eleven years.

In 1978 I put up my own cup - the C.M. Cartwright Cup - in the Dudley Metro Cup Competitions - and I'm glad to say that Celtic won it in our fiftieth anniversary year - the 1993/94 season. What I'm working for now is the chance to have completed sixty years as secretary of the club! I think we made a valuable contribution to the life of Quarry Bank and I think we were a well-loved team but somehow I don't think we quite had the support we deserved, simply because were surrounded by so many semi-professional teams which could command greater support. And, of course there were other local teams like Dunns Bank Rovers and our old rivals in later years - Quarry Bank Rangers - a team that had once been based at the Labour Club. (Football in Quarry Bank was quite non-political - at one time Sid Whitehouse, a Labour councillor was our President, Ewart Bloor, a Liberal, was our Chairman, and I, with my interest in the Conservative Club, was the Secretary! - all three Great Western Railway men.)

Quarry Bankers who were founder members who are still alive are: Messrs. J.T. Robinson, W.R. Cartwright, C. Cooper, C. Evans, W.G. Hamblett, M. Dunn and W. Scott. Men who have helped the committee in early years include the late Arthur Kent, Bill Massey, Bob Walker, Jack Pugh, Arthur Jones, and Bill Lilley. From 1950 until his death in 1984 Sol Pearson was my Assistant Secretary - another Quarry Banker who did a great deal of hard work for QB Celtic.

I have had other interests besides the Celtic - for example I went into local politics and stood as a Conservative candidate in local elections. I am secretary of Quarry Bank Conservative Club, having been a member for forty five years. I've served on the Brighter Old Age Committee and helped organise the Gala, the Coronation Committee, the Community Centre. I've been a school governor for a spell. I've worked 45 years on the railway and was active in the NUR for seventeen years. Everything that I have been involved in I have stayed for a long while and I have always wanted to be actively involved. I've had an interesting life, but my first love has always been the Celtic.

Below: Quarry Bank Celtic F.C. 1947/48, in front of the pavilion in Stevens Park.: Standing: V. Reese, S.Ashmore, R. Jasper, R. Davies, R. Sidaway, & G. Haycock. Fornt: Cyril Carwright, F. Hickman, N. Allen, J. Bloomer (Capt), S. Dunn, R. Saunders, Bill Smith (trainer). Trophies: Corbett Hospital Cup and League Cup.

Below: Q.B. Celtic F.C., the 1993/94 50th Anniversary team.
Standing: W.Hamblett, (Vice President), T. Robinson (President), C. Connop (Committee), then S. Bowen, P. Mc.Phee, N. Dunkley, P. Liptrot, D. Butler, J. Saunders (Asst. Team Manager), A. Martin, L. Palmer, S. Chilton, A. Jones (trainer), Cyril Cartwright.
Front row: L. Mills, K Richard, P. Collins (Cpat), M. Rowley, L Chilton, R. Lees.
Trophy: C. M. Cartwright Cup. awarded by the Metro League.

Dunns Bank Football Club

Charmayne Redding collected this information from **Joe Jones.**

It all began about 1955. The idea of forming the football team came from three men: Joe Jones, Mr. Raybould, and Mr. Thompson. They watched lads playing football and decided to form a club for them. The club went from strength to strength, first being based at the Liberal club and then the New Inns.

The club built up a first and second team and won many cups over the next forty years, but it finished sometime in the mid 1990s.

Below: A Dunns Bank first team of the 1970s:
standing: Joe Jones, B. Turner, ?, A Mullett, G. Nock, T. Cadman, T. Mason, S. Sidaway, R. Jones, and Keith Tomlinson.
Kneeling: M. Cooke, M. Southall, R. Parry, R. Slater, and D. Fellows.

Bottom: A more recent Dunns Bank second team:
Standing: B. Turner, ?, D. Perks, M. Gill, ?, ?, D. Guise, B. Underhill, Joe Jones.
Kneeling: Graham ?, Wayne ?, M. Hills, G. Chance, ?, M. Wood.

Chapter 13
Quarry Bank's People and Characters

The members of the Mount Pleasant Local History Group have often discussed the people and characters most likely to be remembered by Quarry Bankers at the end of the 20th Century. The people remembered range from folks like Edwin Gordon, who was probably only known within Quarry Bank itself, to our local pop stars and footballers whose fame spread further afield.

The simple fact is that we have not been able to include everybody here. If you feel left out, or that your ancestor has been left out, do get in touch with us!

1. Quarry Bank's famous doctors

Dr. Maylett Smith.

Francis Maylett Smith, son of an English clergyman, was educated at St. Paul's School, and St. Mary's Hospital. While at the latter, his training was interrupted by the onset of deafness, which forced him to use a hearing aid for the rest of his life.

He worked as a medical assistant in the South Wales Coalfield from 1908 until 1915. He came to Quarry Bank in 1916, taking over the existing practice at Ingleside in the High Street. What happened next is told from Chapter 9 onwards in his autobiography, "A GP's Progress to the Black Country". The book gives an informative and sometimes amusing account of his experiences in Quarry Bank from 1916 to 1933.

Dr. Maylett Smith felt that Quarry Bankers were less literate and less politically sophisticated than the mining population of South Wales, but his final conclusion was this: "Of all the communities I have known, this was the most amiable and good natured, with a warmth of heart and neighbourly good feeling not easily matched in this imperfect world. ... For all its unconventional ways, Quarry Bank[1] was the politest society I have ever had the good fortune to belong to."

Dr. Maylett Smith died in 1945, in Shropshire, at the age of sixty seven. Although he left Quarry Bank in 1933, there are still many who can remember him. Frank Webb has recalled coming back to Quarry Bank late at night from his work and studies in Birmingham. As he walked up the High Street the doctor would call him in for a drink and to listen to a record played on a gramophone with a huge horn. The doctor never let his deafness interfere with any aspect of getting on with life.

Dr. Kate Rogers

In May 1965 Kate Rogers was standing as Brierley Hill's prospective Labour candidate in the General Election. Joyce Roberts of the Express & Star went along to interview Kate, and her agent Kenneth Taylor. These words are extracted from Joyce Roberts' report:

Everyone knows Kate Rogers. I could see this as soon as I asked the way to her surgery. Ken Taylor explained - "If Dr. Kate walks down Thorns Road, she is greeted by everyone - not just her patients. She is a village personality, and I think most people would feel a certain rapport with her." Maybe it's the combined effect of her personal gusto and impish grin directed at you from a considerable height - and her big 'Ethel Merman' voice.

"I am one of life's unappropriated blessings," Kate chuckled, "being a single woman, and I enjoy my freedom - I do not have to ask my husband's blessing about anything!"

Her politics are another expression of her independent spirit. "I am Labour by conviction, but not by birth. All my family are strong Conservatives."

It was some time after coming from London to take up her present practice in Quarry Bank in 1948 that she found her political feet. Although she had long held strong Socialist sympathies, she had never joined a political party until 1951, when she joined the Brierley Hill constituency of the Labour Party to become a Staffordshire County Councillor. She was elected with a majority of 2,595 - the biggest majority of any county councillor in the country! She has been on the County Council ever since.

Doctor Fair

---

[1] Quarry Bank is called "Colliers Forge" in the book!

How did she explain this first landslide? "I think it was a sort of personality 'thank you' vote to me as their doctor," she said affectionately. In 1964 she joined the Brierley Hill UDC, and is now the first woman Parliamentary candidate for Brierley Hill.

As a woman and a doctor Kate Rogers held strong views on infant welfare clinics and the principle of bringing a variety of local health services under one roof. Between 1952 and 1955 she was vice-chairman of the county health committee and fought for a number of health and welfare issues. In Brierley Hill Dr. Kate joined the Governors of the Grammar School, and in Quarry Bank was a founder-president of the Darby & Joan Club.

"My great hobby is tapestry working. In Christ Church, Quarry Bank, there is a copy of Holman Hunt's "The Light of the World" which I worked in tapestry," said Dr. Kate as she unrolled a beautiful 12 ins square tapestry she had all but finished. "I am also a keen motorist, and have passed the test for advanced motorists." Returning from answering the phone, Dr. Kate showed me an oil painting of the willow-lined canal near Stourton. "My first attempt!" she explained rather surprisingly.

"I like good theatre and classical music. I like to read good novels and political biographies - and I make my own clothes."

"Kate, you've forgotten your jam and marmalade making!" added Ken Taylor. "And it's very nice jam too - it goes well at the bring-and-buy sales."

Doctor Fair.

It was a Spring day in 1948 when Doctor Fair came to live and practise in Quarry Bank. She had attended the London School of Medicine for Women, and then worked in York, where she became friends with Dr. Kate Rogers. They decided to set up practice together, and to the great benefit of the local community, they bought the High Street practice from Dr. McFarlane in Quarry Bank.

Doctor Fair lived with her husband, Major Richard Taylor, above the surgery for many years, bringing up eight children. Her husband supported her by becoming her unofficial practice manager after leaving the Army. Dr. Kate Rogers moved to the surgery in Thorns Road.

Doctor Fair was a good and caring doctor, always ready to listen, to help, and to visit. The children grew up, and in 1980 her husband died. From then on she devoted all her energies into looking after her patients, and was always on call. It was the elderly who were mainly indebted to her - she would call on them as a matter of course whether or not they were ill.

For forty three years Doctor Fair served the people of Quarry Bank faithfully, and was loved by all who came to know her. Latterly she was joined in the practice by Dr. Seeta Siriwardine.

A practising Christian, Dr. Fair played an active part in the life of Christ Church. Sometimes she came into the services late, and on other Sundays had to leave early, but she always attended. She started a club for widows, and was a member of the Iona Community, visiting the island every year.

Many people felt strongly that Dr. Fair should receive the MBE, and she was nominated a number of times. However, she was not to receive the honour she deserved. But, as she said, "I am remembered in the hearts of the patients and community at Quarry Bank, and that's what matters."

Dr. Fair finally retired at the age of seventy five and went to live in Westgate in Kent, and was much missed. However, she has now returned to the Black Country and lives in Kingswinford, regularly visited by her old friends. On 27th June 1999 she attended Rev. Tom Chapman's final service at Christ Church.

----

2. Local Characters

Nurse Green

(Compiled from notes produced by Doreen Cartwright and Olive Allchurch.)

Nurse Green was the District midwife in Quarry Bank for forty years, in which time she attended hundreds of mothers and brought many many Quarry Bankers into the world.

Nurse Ethel Rowley was born on 15th Nov 1891, and trained in Tipton, becoming certified as a mid-wife in June 1915. She began nursing in Quarry Bank in 1916 and delivered her first local baby in February 1916 - for Mrs. Raybould of Oak Street. She also nursed flu victims during the flu epidemic of the First World War. She married in 1920 and became Nurse Green.

On 3rd April 1936 Nurse Green delivered a daughter to Mrs. Morgan. The little girl weighed only one and a half pounds and Doctor McGregor did not think that she would live. In fact he said there would be no charge to Mrs. Morgan if the baby did survive! Nurse Green spent hours at the house, and cleaned the baby with olive oil. Two weeks after the birth the local paper was declaring the the Midlands' smallest baby was doing well and had gained 5 oz. in the last ten days. The baby did survive and in gratitude she was named Ethel after Nurse Green. Young Ethel later died of pneumonia in her twenties but her survival as an infant was quite remarkable in those days.

As well as her career as the local midwife, she was also employed as a school nurse for many years. Nurse Green never drove a car - always walked at her own leisurely pace - and for so many years was one of the best known figures in Quarry Bank. She was always calm and in control - quite unflappable, aware of her own wealth of experience and completely self confident. This self confidence spilled over to many a young mother, and young babies certainly responded to her confident handling. Nurse Green was a true no-nonsense Quarry Bank character.

The last baby she delivered in Quarry Bank was for Mrs. Collins of Birch Avenue in August 1955. Nurse Green herself lived a long life - she died in December 1989 at the age of ninety eight.

Albert Shaw

In the late 1960s the Black Country had a number of "folk clubs" which met regularly in local pubs to enjoy playing and listening to variety of folk-music. This led to an interest in discovering any Black Country traditions and to find singers that could still embody this tradition. The search led to the discovery of such Quarry Bank talents as George Dunn (1887 - 1975). His songs were recorded and his biography was written, but he was really too old a man to take part in presenting his music live to the pub-based audience of the folk-revival. A Quarry Banker who did play a part in that 'scene' was Albert Shaw of Woods Crescent.

Albert Shaw was born in 1908 and attended the Quarry Bank School until leaving at 14 to enter the bucket-bashing trade. He progressed to enamelling, but like many local working men he was frustrated by poor rates of pay in these local trades and a feeling that the work was not secure. He went to Birmingham in search of work and helped build aero-engines when the Second World War began. Later he was a machine gun fitter at a factory in Stallings Lane, Kingswinford. After the War he settled down at The Austin - joining many other men from this part of the Black Country who made their way daily to Longbridge. He became an inspector of gearbox components.

He had always enjoyed singing, but up until the 1960s this had always been within the family circle. His father, Levi Shaw, had sung, and his uncle, Frank Pardoe, had been a whistler of local repute. Albert developed a salty baritone voice and a repertoire of local songs. His sons, who had once preferred Elvis to their father's music, and also worked at the Austin, later became interested in folk music and introduced two local singers to Albert.

Albert's other great interest in life was making home-brewed beer, and a quantity of beer flowed that night Albert met the young folk-singers. The result was an invitation to appear at a local folk club, and from that moment Albert's career as a folk singer "took off". He became a well known figure at clubs throughout the West Midlands.

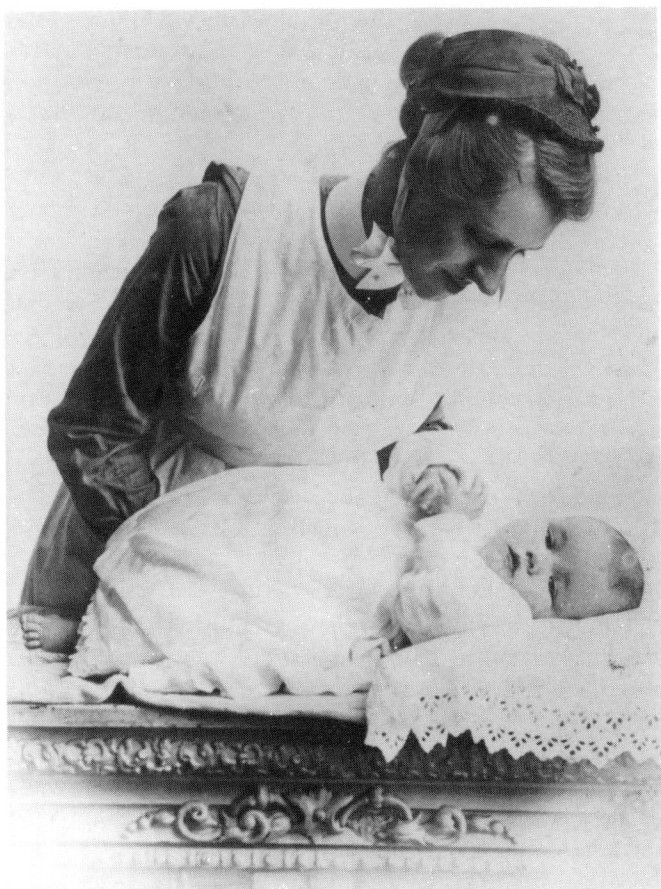

Nurse Green about 1920 + baby Gerald Brown.

Albert Shaw

John Robinson
by Margaret Priest

It's a well known fact in Quarry bank that many of its sons are the salt of the earth, and one excellent example is John Robinson, born in Mount Pleasant some ninety odd years ago.

Before John was born, his mother Ann had been left a widow with six young children, her husband having been tragically killed on the railway. Some years later she met Alfred Robinson, and when he was offered work in Glasgow in a bedstead company she accompanied him to Scotland, taking her three youngest children. As regards the older children, Ann went into service, William went to stay with an uncle in Sheffield, and Albert stayed with an uncle in Watford. They travelled to Scotland by train, and to avoid paying for Lil they wrapped her in a shawl and carried her. The Guard observed dryly: "Bloody old face for a kid that young!"

But Quarry Bank calls its own and when Alfred was offered a job at Peerless Bedstead Company they moved back home. Alfred Thomas Robinson married Ann Rebecca Blewitt on 14th July 1907 and they settled down at No. 10 Mount Pleasant. Just over twelve months later John was born soon followed by Henry and then Sidney.

John well remembers his life as a little lad: no gas or electricity, and one tap between four houses. All the floors were red quarry tiles with fire grates in each room, and the rooms were lit by oil lamps. But the house was roomy with four bedrooms, as they had space above the wide entry. On the ground floor, beyond the fode, was a brewhouse/bakehouse and a two storey workshop, some of which was used to keep pigs in the First World War, and was later used by Charlie Hollis, a boatman, to stable his horse. The family lived in this house until John was about ten, and then they moved across the road to a house which was next door but one to The Brickmaker's Arms.

As a lad, John was never idle. Money was earned fetching coal from Dews End coal merchants in the Delph and he regularly delivered to houses in Amblecote Road - particularly to nos. 79 and 81 - both of which are still standing. For this he was given 2d a barrow. Next to Freda Price's shop was Dickens the barbers and every night and most Saturdays would find John lathering the customers. When required he would also fetch a pot of tea from Mrs. Homer's, from over the road. The only thing that kept John away from work was his beloved football - if playing for the school his brother Henry would have to "stand in" for him.

By the time John was ten he was to be found on Sundays blowing the organ at the Wesleyan Chapel. He also had a good singing voice, and was asked to join the choir at Christ Church where Joseph Bloomer was the choirmaster and organist. However, the £2 a year he earned blowing the organ was more useful so he forfeited the chance to join the choir. Anyway - he could sing while doing his job! John once asked to be paid every four weeks instead of annually, but when the new treasurer, Don Warwick, queried the thirteen payments he decided to leave - and changed his allegiance to Brierley Hill Church.

While John had been at Mount Pleasant School, Gaffer Hunt was the Headmaster. John was good at his studies, but excelled at sports, particularly boxing, athletics and football After leaving school he was in the Old Boys Team. Later, as he grew up, cross country running became a favourite pastime, and he joined Dudley Harriers.

At school John had helped the caretaker, Felix Penn, sweep up and clean windows. Felix, who had been gassed in the First World War, was often unwell and John gradually took over more responsibilities. At that time John's father was doing casual work at Roberts & Cooper's in Mill Street so when he was offered the caretaker's job, he was delighted to accept it - Felix Penn being too unwell to continue. The job involved all the family - with Ann doing cleaning and John and his brothers helping in any way they could. Mr. Robinson was renowned for the excellent beer he brewed, and young John often took some into school to help the teachers survive the day.

After leaving school John went to work at the Jury, and continued the study of woodwork at nightschool - four nights a week! Under the expert tuition of Mr. John Brookes he learned to make furniture - from sideboards to bedsteads. At the Jury he made mounted forgings, and later became an enamel fuser - during the War this was a reserved occupation.

With his many interests he somehow found time to court Irene Thorneycroft from Brockmoor. They saved every penny they could so that when they married - when John was 26 - they were able to buy their own house. For this John purchased 500 sq.yds of land at the top of the Thorns at the cost of 5/- per sq.yd. He made a contract with Frank Webb to build the house, and with Sidney's expert help as painter and decorator, and his brother-in-law doing the wiring, he saved a significant amount. John made his own newell posts and furniture - and furnished his brothers' homes. In 1934 he completed his new detached home for £425.

John and Irene settled down in The Thorns - Irene worked as a glass maker at Webb Crystal and John continued to work at the Jury. The Thorns was a quiet road in those days. Hill's Farm was situated nearby and milk from the cows was delivered by the farmer's wife. During the war, John cultivated land behind his house - growing much needed vegetables, and later bought this 100yd stretch from the Council.

After working at the Jury for some years, John needed a

change and therefore applied for a job with the MEB. Initially he was given a job of delivering accounts, but soon became a meter reader working over a very wide area. John retired from the MEB at sixty five - feeling that he had never tired of the job, having always enjoyed meeting people from all walks of life. Even in retirement there would never be enough hours in the day for all his interests - gardening, woodworking, and the church. John had been Vicar's warden at Brockmoor Church for twenty one years.

John now lives in Brockmoor, and is still very active in mind and body - his interests still include woodworking and gardening, walking, reading, listening to the radio and politics. He has been an active member of the Mount Pleasant Local History Group where he has been able to provide first hand information about the history of Mount Pleasant School, as an ex-pupil and about the caretaking. His knowledge of local industry and the people of bygone Quarry Bank has also been invaluable.

John's philosophy of life is: "Be good to others and they'll be good to you, but don't be afraid to stand up for your principles should the need arise." - A true Quarry Banker.

Left: John Robinson.

Below: Mary Southall is second from the left on the front row, among her contemporaries attending Christ Church, Quarry Bank.

Mary Southall

Mary Southall's family on the maternal side could be traced back to the Greens who were cousins to the Richardsons and the Guests. Her grandmother was Mary Anne Green who was born in Wordsley, and married James Southall. Mary Anne had a wonderful contralto voice and could play the concertina. Mary Southall was born with a fine soprano voice, and even at the age of five could sing beautifully. She was brought up in Quarry Back by her grandparents, who encouraged her musical talents. James Southall and his wife lived in one of the houses behind the Blue Ball in Quarry Bank and James' musical skills extended to being able to repair and build musical instruments. At one time, it seems, he had been musical director on Bostock & Wombell's famous travelling menagerie show.

Mary sang solo in Christ Church - singing "Angels ever Bright and Fair", while standing on a stool so that everybody could see her, and later joined the Sunday School Ladies Fellowship - as seen in the photograph.

Mary's uncle, Tom Southall, who lived in London sent a critic up to Quarry bank to hear his niece perform. The critic was Edward McNulty - who stayed with Rev Mc-Nulty at the vicarage while in Quarry Bank. Their names were the same but they were not related. On 26 March 1895 Edward McNulty wrote a testimonial for Mary stating that he found her to have a rich soprano voice, singing a high B natural with comparative ease, and commended her musical memory. All this was in aid of sending Mary to the Guild Hall School of Music in London.

She studied for three years at The Guild Hall, and her tutor, Mr. Bright felt she had an assured future singing anything from opera to oratorio. However it was not to be - Mary gave up her career to marry Zacharia Grainger with whom she had been corresponding ever since meeting him as a choirboy. Uncle Tom Southall never really forgave Mary for throwing away her career.

Zacharia Grainger was engineman at Nagersfield Colliery, a job in which he followed in his father's footsteps. He and Mary married at Netherton Church, and Mary went on to have nine children, all of whom were musical. Even so, she never entirely neglected her own musical talents, and at the age of forty she won a gold watch for her singing at the Queens Hall in Brierley Hill. Unfortunately the watch was probably pawned as the family struggled through hard times during the mining disputes of 1921.

The whole family's singing talents became well known and their appearances much appreciated in pubs, clubs, and in chapels and churches on Sundays, and of course they joined local choirs and musical societies. Although remarkably self-trained, members of the family also received help and encouragement from Joseph Bloomer, the organist and choirmaster at Christ Church, Quarry Bank. Mary devoted her life to bringing up her happy and talented family - but, who knows, she might have become a world famous soprano from Quarry Bank.

Cyril and Millie Powell
By Margaret Priest

No one seems to have sat down and worked out how many Quarry Bankers have been included in the Honours Lists over the years. As far as it is known a life peer has never chosen to enter the House of Lords as Lord Quarry Bank - but there may be several local people working towards doing so in the future! Cyril Powell has lived in Quarry Bank for sixty years and was given the MBE in 1960 for work in education.

The beginning of the story goes back to 2nd August 1907 - the day Cyril was born in the Welsh village of Abertilly. He was a bright lad academically, excelled in sports, and played rugby for the Three Counties. Meanwhile Millie Lavinia Case was growing up in Colley gate. Her grandparents lived in Cradley Forge, and Grandpa Deeley gave land for for the chapel there. Millie's father was a tailor's cutter, and to make ends meet during the depression, with his wife's help, he made butchers' aprons which he took round the local shops to sell.

And so, in the fullness of time, Cyril and Millie grew up and both trained as teachers and came to work at Orchard Lane Elementary Boys School where they met in 1930. They married in 1932 and lived for a while in Red Hill, Stourbridge, before moving to Quarry Bank. It was Easter 1939 when they settled into "Gilder's Bungalow" at the lower end of Thorns Road. Anthony

was born the following July, and then Vivienne in 1945.

Cyril Powell took a post at the Blue Coat School in Dudley teaching science and maths. The War started and after a stint in the ARP, he joined the Air Force. He was transferred from the Air Force to the Education Corps in the Army because of his knowledge of radar. Just before the War he had applied for the position of Headmaster at Stambermill but had been unsuccessful. Six years later - returning from the Forces - he once more applied for that job, and this time he was accepted. He was just thirty six years old.

Millie continued her career as a teacher at Valley Road School and then at Shenstone Emergency Training College as a lecturer in the Art Department. Later Millie became a Senior Lecturer in Art at a new teacher training college near Kidderminster.

After spending nine years at Stambermill, Cyril Powell was offered the position of Headmaster at Gigmill School. This was a new school with forward thinking progressive ideas. Music was on the curriculum and an orchestra was formed which was quite a radical innovation at the time. Despite scepticism the orchestra went on to do very well, and Gigmill became well known throughout the the country for its excellence - leading to Cyril being awarded the MBE.

Cyril had attained his Licenciate of the London College of Music, and after retiring from school was persuaded to take up teaching the piano. Now in his 92nd year, he still has pupils, and many children and adults have happy memories of music lessons and lasting friendships formed.

Having lived in Quarry Bank since 1939, Cyril and Millie have memories of Thorns Road as being almost a country road: single carriageway and with no proper footpath. A ditch ran alongside the road with slabs of Rowley Rag placed across it at intervals. The house in which the Powells live was previously owned by Grocers who had a shop in High Street, opposite Sheffield Street. It had a large garden stretching the length of what is now Brandon Way. After the war, two PoWs from a house in Woods Lane came to help cultivate it. Next door was Ernest Stevens' (John's nephew) bungalow. In his garden were large sheds filled with "seconds" and "thirds" from the factory. Although it was quiet in Thorns Road, one was reminded of the existence of The Jury when the shifts changed - suddenly the road was full of hustle and bustle. An air raid shelter had been built between the two houses - years later this was used to build rockeries.

Cyril and Millie Powell are still living in Thorns Road, both very active, outgoing, and in touch with life, although it now seems so different. When asked about his long life, so much of which has been spent in Quarry Bank, Mr. Powell thought for a bit, smiled, and said, "It isn't over yet!"

Above: Councillor Ralph Homer
(Elsie Payne Collection)

Above: Ernest Stevens, John Henry Stringer and Ralph Homer at the inauguration of the bandstand in Stevens Park on 22nd August 1925. (Elsie Payne Collection)

Ralph Homer

Ralph Homer lived in Quarry Bank all his life (1884 to 1965), and was well known for his contribution to the work of Cradley Forge Methodist Church, and as a local councillor.

After leaving school Ralph Homer went to work for Ernest Stevens Ltd. at Cradley Heath and worked his way up to Departmental Foreman. He stayed there for his entire working life. At Ernest Stevens' works he became involved with the Workpeople's Hospital Committee and became Secretary of that committee in January 1919. This became quite a time-demanding job both in raising funds for local hospitals, and helping workers meet their health needs. In 1930 he was given a presentation mahogany secretaire in recognition of the work he had been doing.

He became a fully accredited local preacher in 1907, and became Sunday School Superintendent at Cradley Forge, as well as becoming one of the church trustees. He was also an ardent temperance worker and presided over a 200-strong branch of the Band of Hope. It seems only fitting that Ralph should marry a preacher's daughter. In 1911 he married Miss Minnie Worton - the daughter of Caleb Worton of Cradley Heath. The Homers had two daughters - Maud and Elsie.

He was also involved with the "Early Morning Adult School" which provided an educational opportunity for working men anxious to improve their basic education and who could only find time to take up such opportunities early on Sunday mornings.

In 1921 Ralph became Vice Chairman of the Public Park & War Memorial Committee that was set up, under the chairmanship of James Dunn, to look into developing a park and war memorial on land generously given to the town by Ernest Stevens.

When a branch of the Labour Party was formed after the First World War, Ralph joined and was successfully elected to the Urban District Council in 1922 - the first year that the Labour Party gained seats on the Council. In April 1928 he became the Council's first Labour Chairman. When the Urban District Council was wound up in 1934, Ralph Homer did not continue this aspect of his work by seeking to join Brierley Hill Council, but he continued his work as a Justice of the Peace, having joined the Bench in 1929. He was also a Conservator of Kinver Common.

In 1948 a plaque was unveiled at Cradley Forge Methodist church to commemorate the outstanding work of three men who had given years of service to the church: David Hadlington, Ralph Homer, and his brother Henry. (See Quarry Bank in Old Photographs - page 53.)

(Most of this information was supplied by Elsie Payne)

John Henry Stringer

John Henry Stringer was born at the Fountain Inn, Victoria Road, Quarry bank on 8th November 1868. He left school at eleven to join his father at the Brockmoor Ironworks, but later entered the holloware trade by joining John Stevens at the works in Brick Kiln Street.

He turned his attention from galvanising to enamelling - in which he became very skilled, and ultimately he became Manager of the Making Up Department at John Stevens' Thorns Road works. He left this post in 1916 to establish his own business - the Tubular Holloware Company (See page 23).

In 1922 John Henry successfully stood for election to the Urban District council as a Labour candidate, and three years later he polled a record number of votes in being elected to the local seat on Staffordshire County Council - defeating Sam Yardley. He also retained the seat on the UDC with a massive show of support. He had to retire from local politics three years later as a result of health problems, but by then he had already made his mark.

On the local council he took charge of the Parks Committee, and cut the first sod for the erection of the bandstand, donated by Ernest Stevens. He pushed hard to bring about the erection of the Peace Memorial, although it was not completed until after his death.

He had always been involved in local charitable work. He had taken over the work of the old Friendly Societies Parades Committee after the War and helped it reorganise itself into what became the Hospital Carnival Committee - responsible for fund-raising and fetes and galas between the Wars.

He was also very much a family man, and he and his wife Nellie had seven children. He loved his garden and grew many flowers at his home in Oak Street. He was never seen without a flower in his button hole. When he moved to a house in Upper High Street he called it "Verbena" after his favourite flower.

His retirement from politics in 1928 was a result of his heart problems, and he did not enjoy good health from thereon. He was forced to take rest despite his love of being involved in public life. In August 1930 he distributed the prizes at the horticultural show held alongside the hospital carnival and gala, although he was by then very ill.

He died a few weeks later on 27th September 1930. As would be expected, his funeral was a major event in Quarry Bank - supported by large deputations from his workforce, his associates in public life, the Labour movement and the ordinary people of Quarry Bank. Some remembered him as an employer or a political figure, others remembered the boiled sweets he used to make on Sundays to distribute to the elderly attending church. The funeral was almost like a state occasion.

Businesses closed down, blinds were drawn and crowds passed through his home to pay their last respects as he lay in his coffin. He was buried in the Christ Church churchyard.

In May 1931 a photograph of J.H. Stringer was unveiled in the Quarry Bank Labour Club as a memorial to the man who had done so much to establish the party in the area and to be its successful candidate at local council and county council level. Charlie Sitch, the first Labour MP to represent the area, could not be there but tributes were made to Mr. Stringer by Wilf Shaw and Simeon Wood. Alf Workman, Mr. Stringer's son-in-law, replied on behalf of the family. (Alf himself became a local councillor.)

The Hospital Carnival Committee, which took over the work of the old Friendly Societies Parade Committee led by Mr. Westwood before the First World War.
John Henry Stringer is standing on the extreme left of the middle row. Other "famous" Quarry Bankers can also be seen such as Frank Webb (Snr) and John Genner.
The location is the Infants School playground but the date is uncertain.
(Emmie Jones Collection)

Right: A youthful Ralph Homer stands to the left of the members of the Quarry Bank "Early Morning School" Class B, about 1905.

Right: Oak Villa in Oak Street - the home of the Stringer Family: Harold, Mrs. Nellie Stringer, Mr. John Henry Stringer, Hilda. Dolly, May, Anne, Nell, Gladys and Elsie. (See pages 4 & 23)

(Olwen Homer Colln.)

Right: Inside the new library, in February 1939, the civic party remove their hats but not their coats! Left to right: Wilf Shaw, Ralph Homer, Mr. Edwards (Chairman of Brierley Hill UDC Library Committee), Alf Workman, Mr. A Dudley, and Simeon Wood.

(Top and bottom picture: Elsie Payne's Collection)

89

The Webb Family

As told by Doris to Margaret Priest

My grandparents, Bill and Louie Webb and their family, had always lived in caravans. Before moving to Quarry Bank in 1945, they were based at Netherend, and for a while, the caravans were parked on land at the back of Thorns Public house. Then Grandad Webb bought the land adjoining the Stour at the end of Caledonia. He paid for it with a bucket full of gold sovereigns! At first there were only a couple of caravans - Grandad's and ours, and then more of the family came to live here too.

Bill and Louie had brought up eight children: my Dad, also named Bill, was the eldest son, and the other boy was John. The girls were called Annie, Carrie, Maudie, Alice, Nora, and the youngest was Louie. Louie was about eighteen when the family came to Quarry Bank.

My Dad had married Alice and had two children by the time we came to Quarry Bank - John and myself. My younger sister Alice was born a few years later.

In the beginning we lived in the caravans, but then the Council insisted that we must build "proper" houses. So the first house was built for Gran and Grandad, and then huts for the rest of the family. It was very strange at first for us - especially sleeping - we were so used to being close together in our cosy little home.

All our caravans were beautiful; carved wooden beds, red crystal chandeliers, shining brasses and crocheted lace cloths, and the white metal stove of course. I remember Dad painting the gold leaf on the scrolled panelling.

The men made a living partly by buying and selling scrap metal. Grandad made pegs to sell door to door; he also made wire horseshoe baskets for eggs which were sold to local grocers. Wooden baskets were made too. He used to sit on the steps of the caravan, working away. Louie, my Grandma, made paper flowers. She too preferred working in the open air and made friends with many a passer-by. She loved the children, and often gave a flower to a little one passing with their Mum, who'd paused for a chat.

Every September we went hop picking near Worcester, and then plum picking at Evesham. Of course we went in the caravans, which were parked near the job, so we were able to enjoy the comforts of our own home. One year we brought back six hop vines which we planted: they grew really well!

Our horses have always been important to our families. When we were on the road with the caravans they were indispensable. The two I particularly remember were called 'Showman' and 'Prince', who took us hop picking.

Sunshine bungalow was built in the middle sixties for my Mum and Dad, and it's been my home ever since. Another bungalow for Alice, my sister, and her husband Alf was built more recently.

My Gran was such a well-known person in Quarry Bank, people still mention her, and my Uncle John too, who went everywhere on his bike. The old caravans were all sold a long time ago, but we still keep our horses. And I've got such wonderful memories of the old days.

Louie Webb, Doris's grandmother.

Bill and Alice Webb

3. Quarry Bank Hall of Fame

Keith & Tony West

In the 1990s world of disco dancing, karaoke and computer generated entertainment it is difficult to remember a time, not so long ago, when pubs and clubs provided a wealth of live entertainment - music, comedy and song provided by local people for local people. Most pubs had a piano and there was always a pianist to hand to accompany any volunteer singers, or invited "artistes"

The brothers, Tony and Keith Tomlinson, of Dunns Bank, grew up in this world and made their debut in such an environment. Keith first sang for an audience in his Grandfather's pub - The Old Farm, at Harts Hill - and a hat was passed round to make a collection for him. The first time the brothers sang together in public was at The Hope & Anchor in Bower Lane on a Saturday night towards the end of the 1950s. They sang "Oh My Papa", and Tony was about twenty, Keith was about fourteen.

Tony joined the Quarry Bank Operatic Society just as it was becoming established at the new Community Centre, and took part in the "Midsummer Madness" revue and "Winterland" revue put on in the early 1960s. Keith also joined and played the lead in about five shows.

It was about that time that they sang together at one of Old Hill Labour Club's "free & easy" evenings. Someone invited them to come back and appear as an "act", for which they would get paid. Up until that moment they had presented themselves very informally and hadn't actually thought of themselves as an "act". Now they had become "Tony & Keith" and they had to think about selecting material and presenting it. Gran knitted them some new matching sweaters: one pair for their first appearance, one pair for the second!

Things began to snowball - they were invited to sing at other pubs and clubs. They began to learn about the business and developed their own style. They sang a variety of material: popular songs, songs from the shows, ballads and Country & Western numbers, so it was not the material that made them uniquely "Tony & Keith" - it was more the sound that they created by singing in close harmony. They harmonised naturally, their voices blending together in an attractive way which never seemed contrived. Although they had no trouble singing with each other, they occasionally had trouble working with the chord sequences provided by accompanying musicians! This was solved when a local musician, Tom Watts, joined them as musical director. He stayed with them for many years and eventually became musical director of the MWM Show. Gradually elements of the act were brought under control by using their own sound. An agent in Birmingham suggested that they adopt the stage name "West".

As the 1960s unfolded their "fame" spread and they worked further and further afield. Occasionally the club world produced a tough audience but generally the work was pleasurable and audiences were good. "There were more good nights than bad nights", recalls Tony. They were frequently re-booked, and joined shows where they appeared nightly for a whole week. Although their stage work now took them all over the country to theatres and clubs, they never gave up their "day jobs" and never severed contact with Quarry Bank and surrounding area.

In a supporting role, they appeared in shows featuring stars such as Marti Cain, Paul Daniels, Frank Carson, Paul Jones, The Searchers, Gerry & The Pacemakers, Stan Stennett, Harry H. Corbett, David Whitfield and Ann Shelton. They auditioned a couple of times for "Opportunity Knocks", without success.

In the early 1970s an agent suggested that they audition for "Opportunity Knocks" again. They went along to the Midland Hotel in Birmingham for an audition and were told immediately that they had been selected. The first appearance on the show was recorded on 12th October 1974 and was broadcast a few days later. In the first heat they knocked Tom O'Connor, from his top position, and went on to appear in four more shows.

Their career really took off at this point - but they still remained semi-professional. They signed a three year recording contract with EMI and went down to London to make a single in the Abbey Road studios, where the Beatles had recorded many of their famous songs. The "A" side was "I Understand", a number previously recorded by Freddie & The Dreamers, and the "B" side was "Bridge Over Troubled Waters". These numbers were given the full recording studio treatment and the brothers' harmonies were backed by the Mike Sams Singers and a 36 piece orchestra!

Needless to say, the record shot to number one in the local charts - and sold in great numbers at Deeley's Record Shop, in Cradley Heath. There was a moment when it seemed poised to enter the national charts and there was talk of an appearance on Top of the Pops. If this had happened Tony & Keith might have had to even give up their day jobs! Fate intervened however, and within a few days of the record being released, Tony electrocuted himself on stage when grabbing a "live" microphone.

While recuperating in early 1975, Tony also found that he had been made redundant from his "day job", EMI seemed to lose interest in further recordings, and the brothers seemed to find themselves reconsidering their career almost as soon as it had seemed they were on the road to stardom. The outcome of all this was that Tony and Keith joined in the formation of the "MWM Show".

The MWM Show was a complete stage "package" taking its name from the initials of the seven participants: The Wests, plus Tom Watts (organist), Linda Marsh (vocalist), Tommy Mundon (Comic), George Willets (drummer), and Horace Mackay (compere). Putting on the MWM Show occupied the next ten years of Tony's and Keith's lives - sometimes working harder than they had worked before. (And yet it was a time when Keith also managed the Dunns Bank Football Club team, and still appeared in the Operatic Society's shows. Tony drove the group's van and humped the equipment around.

The shows were much more "theatrical" than anything the brothers had presented before - with costume changes, dance routines and set pieces, in which Ken Allen played a key producer's role. Each November the Civic Hall at Brierley Hill was booked for four nights and a "new" show was presented, which then toured other venues for the next twelve months, on what became a regular "circuit". The tour would often include a long run at Westley Court where the show formed an after-meal cabaret. The show's set piece was often a "tribute", for example a tribute to the songs of Frank Sinatra, or the music of Disney's films. A particularly successful set was called "Tribute to a Dream" which featured a selection of Second World War songs.

The launch of each new show at the Civic Hall was always a sell-out, but they sold their own tickets and programmes - therefore needing administrative support from folks like Tony's wife, Lyn. The brothers also made their own LPs which they sold themselves. Keith "retired" in 1985, but Tony carried on for another three years with the Tommy Mundon Show.

The Tony and Keith "Story" seems to revolve around the moment when they might have become nationally known chart-toppers. The fact that they returned to a much more local scene after that moment - and after Tony's accident - preserved them in the role that has probably endeared them to their local fans. Tony still lives in Quarry Bank, and Keith still lives in Cradley Heath - they are still local lads!

Below: The MWM show

M.W.M. Stage Show

Opposite page: Left: Joe Tate
Right: Trevor Smith
(Sheila Marshall Collection)

Joe Tate (1904 - 1973)

Articles on the career of Joe Tate, written by Dennis Shaw, appeared in Claret & Blue in November 1993 and September 1995; the latter as a result of an interview with Nellie Tate.

Joe Tate was born 4th August 1904 in Old Hill. Later he lived in Bower Lane, Quarry Bank.

Between 1927 and 1934 Joe Tate played for Aston Villa on nearly two hundred occasions, later telling his wife Nellie, "When I played for Aston Villa I was the happiest man in the world, because they are the greatest club in the world". He became a footballing legend as part of the half-back line of Gibson, Talbot & Tate.

Tate also donned an England shirt on 14th May 1931 to play against France in Paris - gaining four full England caps altogether. After playing against Belgium and Wales, he was selected to play against Austria in December 1932, but he sustained an injury shortly before the match and his international career was over. He never really recovered from the injury and his club career ended in 1934. At the age of 31 he left league football to become player manager of Brierley Hill.

In 1936 he broke his neck while playing for Brierley Hill and his playing days were over altogether. He went into a tobacconist business in Brierley Hill.

Trevor Smith

Notes by Roy Smith.

Trevor Smith was born in the heart of the Black Country at Quarry Bank on 13th April 1936. He played for Quarry Bank Secondary Modern Boys School, and joined Birmingham City as an amateur in July 1951, turning professional in April 1953.

Trevor enjoyed some great days in the years from 1951 to 1956. In 1951, as the Captain of Brierley Hill & Sedgley Schools F.A. team, he gained a runners up medal in the England Schools' Trophy Final. He was in the Blues side which won the European Youth Cup in Switzerland in 1952. A year later he won a permanent place in Birmingham's League team. In 1955 he helped the Blues win the Second Division Championship, and played for England "B" and Under 23s.

In 1956 Trevor played at Wembley in the FA Cup final against Manchester City. One of his team mates in the England Under 23s team was Dudley's Duncan Edwards. Trevor went on to become a fine centre half, serving the Blues for eleven years.

Although Army service disrupted his progress in the mid 1950s, Trevor went on to win two England Full Caps against Wales and Sweden in 1959, as a replacement for Billy Wright. A year later he played in the final Inter-cities Fairs Cup, now known as the UEFA Cup, and in 1963 he collected a winner's prize in the League Cup Final.

During the late 1950s, Trevor skippered the Blues, but in 1958 he thought of leaving St. Andrews, reasoning that a change of club might benefit his career. Instead he stayed another six years before transferring to Walsall in October 1964 for the princely sum of £18,000.

Retiring from football in February 1966, Trevor and his wife, Mary, now run a pub in Dagenham, Essex. In the Charles Buchan Soccer Gift Book 1957-58, Trevor is quoted as saying: "So many honours came my way between my fifteenth and twentieth birthdays that I sometimes think it is all a dream."

Tommy Jennings

As a child Tommy lived across the Amblecote Road and was able to walk or cycle to Mount Pleasant School. His interest in cycling may have started at Mount Pleasant while in Mr. Allchurch's class. On Friday afternoons Mr. Allchurch ran a form lesson in which Tommy used to volunteer to clean the teachers' bikes. He thinks it was D'Arcy Jones' bike that he usually cleaned. His own bike was one that his Aunt had bought - after his father had failed to win him one at the fair.

Tommy later went to Quarry Bank Boys Secondary School in Coppice Lane and cycled to school every day. The family then moved to Victoria Road and he became friendly with the Whylies who were keen cyclists: Billy, Vic and Ron who was the same age as Tommy. Vic was a member of the Halesowen Athletics and Cycling Club - the cycling section being formed in 1943. Tommy joined in 1944, and won a hill-climbing championship.

Just as Tommy's interest in cycling was beginning to take off, he was called-up only to find that he was to become a "Bevin Boy" and was to be sent off to Hilton Main Colliery. This rather curtailed his training, but in 1946 he was transferred to the Turk Colliery at the Delph - one of Tinker Round's pits. Not only was this pit "local", but Tommy also found that he only had to work a seven-till-twelve shift, which gave him time to resume his training. When he was demobbed he went to work at Sammy Taylors.

By 1947 the time-trial scene was dominated by the Halesowen Club - using a stretch of the Coventry Road at Stonebridge on the far side of Birmingham. This involved a twenty five mile ride over to Stonebridge before taking part in the trials. The North Worcestershire Road Racing Club was re-started and Bill Whylie and Tommy joined and started winning local team events. In 1948 Bill went back to the Halesowen Club which gave Tommy a free rein at the North Worcs. club.

In 1949 Tommy went back for a short spell of track racing at Halesowen and then took up open-road racing, riding in international competitions. Those days were the "golden years" of cycle racing - before cars pushed cycling off the road.

Now Tommy is in the Veteran Cycling Club.

Tommy never knew he had a Quarry Bank accent until one day while on a cycle tour of Scotland. He and his friends were looking for bed and breakfast accommodation near Loch Lomond. He went into the Post Office to ask for advice. After he had spoken a voice from the back of the Post Office boomed, "And do the women in Cradley Heath still make chain at the bottom of the garden?"

Above: Young Tommy Jennings and his friend Bill Whylie.

Below: The North Worcs. Road Racing Club. Tommy Jennings is fourth from the right in the middle row.
(Both pictures from Tommy Jennings' Collection)

Chapter 14
Personal Memoirs

Jesse Yorke

As a little girl I came to live in Thorns Road in the 1920s when it was very different to the busy thoroughfare that it is today. There was no deep drainage and the ditches on either side of the road carried stale smelly water - a breeding place for germs. Diphtheria was a common yet dreaded childhood disease: both my brother Victor, and I caught it.

As the grand-daughter of William Stevens, the elder brother of John and Ernest, The Jury was to play an important part in our childhood. My Dad, Bert Stevens, worked there. We loved to watch our road come to life as the shifts changed at The Jury. There was plenty for us to see, as the furnaces worked round the clock, and it was exciting to see lorries coming in and out of the works. During the school holidays I was allowed to help pack enamel ware, a great treat for a little girl of eight or so!

Thorns Road was a close community in its own right, away from the village. Everyone helped one another without being intrusive. On Sunday evenings the men could be seen in straw-brimmed hats strolling up to The Blue Ball. No ladies were allowed to accompany them - although they may have been treated to a visit to the pictures in Stourbridge on Saturday night!

Most of my playmates were boys and they made me 'keep cave' when they were up to mischief. I used to trail after the lads to the pools at Hill's Farm at the top of the Thorns, where we had great fun fishing with a stick and a bent pin, or it was possible to go skating there in the winter. It was possible to go over the wall from Mount Pleasant School - which I attended - straight into Hill's Farm and play our way home through the 'Twelve Acres'.

On our walks down Woods Lane it was deliciously frightening to race past Polly Skelding's. She did have a black cat - but she also had flowers in her window and a bowl of fruit. I remember that she sold apples from her orchard - or, at least, she sold the ones that hadn't been scrumped.

One of my jobs - I would have only been six or seven at the time - was to fetch the milk from Josh Gill's farm at Gayfield - over the Amblecote Road. One day while carrying an overflowing enamel can (from The Jury, of course), I was chased by the cows. I can't remember how much milk was left when I got back home, but I do know I did it in record time.

When the Peace Memorial was opened in Stevens Park I was watching the proceedings from outside the enclosure which held the VIPs. Joseph Bloomer, organist at Christ Church, was leading the choir when suddenly the wind whipped off his wig. Realising what had happened I managed to grab the errant hair-piece as it flew past, and returned it to its owner. Unfortunately I was not allowed to escape and was made to hold the music for the remainder of the performance. It didn't strike me as funny at the time, but I've had many a chuckle since!

Happy Days!

Below: Thorns Road, Quarry Bank, about 1910. The road is a single carriageway carrying relatively light traffic by today's standards! Stevens Park had not been laid out at this time.
(A John Price postcard collected by Marie Billingham)

Madge Richards

I was born in 1922 at my parents' shop at 172 Quarry Bank High Street. (My brother was also born there.) My mother had started the shop in about 1919 - at the end of the First World War. She was a farmer's daughter. My father had been in the War from 1914 to 1918. They were married while he was on leave towards the end of the War, but he had to go back and was very ill. While he was away Mum thought she would rent the shop - and started business with five shillings worth of sweets.

Mum and Dad worked very hard and I was brought up to believe that the shop was very important. There was no skiving in my day! The shop really consisted of two shops - which they ultimately bought. Down through a big entry there were three cottages and a chain shop. Later they moved to another shop a few doors away at 180 High Street. These premises also included some cottages at the back and they were sold to Birds - the butchers.

The business was completely run by Mother - my father was an engineer and refused to have anything to do with the shops. He worked at Barnsley's, and even worked for them for nothing after they had gone bankrupt! Having started off with the sweets Mother went into drapery. She sold everything. If folks wanted a carpet they would come to Mother and she would get it for them. They would pay a shilling a week or whatever - a forerunner of modern hire-purchase! As Jack and I grew up our job on a Friday night was to go "money-hunting" - going to see people who had not been into the shop to pay their weekly dues. I hated going round asking for the money, but we had to do it. This must have been from about the age of ten onwards, because when I left school at fourteen, I couldn't get away from the shop fast enough!

One or two people assisted my mother in the shop - they weren't proper assistants as such, but just used to come and help out when required. For example one lady would look after the shop when my mother went into Birmingham.

My brother went to King Edward School, but there wasn't enough money to send me - I was just a girl and was expected to get married. So I went to school in Quarry Bank until I went to work in Birmingham at Wilkinson Riddells - the big wholesale warehouse from which my mother used to buy her stock. I also started attending the Birmingham School of Commerce as a part time student. I had to catch the train from Cradley Heath early in the morning, after running all the way to the station. The porter was very good - he always held the door of the last carriage open for me. I don't think my parents got very fat on what I earned - I spent it all on clothes!

We had a wonderful time - there was a big crowd of us - and up until the outbreak of War we went everywhere together. It started at the Sunday School, and extended through the Tennis Club, and then we met up with folks from Amblecote Cricket Club. We went to all the dances that were going, from Dudley Town Hall to Stourbridge Town Hall. We would have to walk our way home - especially after the War started.

Jack Cox was part of this crowd, and his mother also had a little shop in Quarry Bank - he was always a popular member of the crowd because he was a little better off and he had a car. We had regular nights when we would all go to the Coronet - everyone had to buy their own tickets, so it was very much a case of "meet you inside". The Coronet changed its programme half way through the week, so we usually went twice a week.

(I didn't really register the Coronet being built, but I can remember the horse paddock that used to be on that site before the cinema, because I used to walk past it on my way down to my Grandparents' farm.)

Although we were such a great crowd socially, nearly everyone married someone who was not in the Quarry Bank crowd. I married Ray Richards from Old Hill at the age of twenty. I met him at Quarry Bank Sunday School. I was married at Quarry Bank Church in 1942 - following in the footsteps of my parents. Later my daughter married at the same church.

The main memory of the War years concerns the time we were evacuated. My father was a veteran of the First World War and he didn't think much of the Second World War. He tended to think the war experience of the ARP folks was fairly mild compared with his experiences. Our house was so far set back from the road, behind large gates. If we were listening to the radio we certainly couldn't hear what was going on in the High Street. The first we knew that anything was going on in Quarry Bank was when my brother returned home from the Coronet. Instead of being able to walk up the High Street he had been forced to make a detour to get home.

My brother came in and said, "Look at you just sitting here - there's a land mine just down the High Street." My father turned to him and said, "Just look at the time! A land mine, indeed. It's probably a cap of a shell in somebody's garden. Get to bed!"

Later my father went to lock the gate and go for a stroll with the dog. When he got to the top of the High Street the ARP wardens said, "Where have you come from?"

"Jack's come home with some story about a land mine, what's going on?"

"There isn't one land mine, there's two, and everybody else has gone. You're supposed to be evacuated."

Dad came back and told us what was going on. It was not long before Christmas and Mum had a house full of money collected for the Christmas Clubs, so naturally she wanted to take that with her, and then they decided to look for the deeds to the house. Then Mother wouldn't go without the canary. We'd got the old dog but we couldn't find the cat, which was fortunate otherwise Mother would have wanted to take it with us. Mother had bought me a fur cape for Christmas, so I had to put that on, as well as Mother's fur. It was some time before we were ready to set off on foot for the home of one of the women who came to the shop. I'm sure we must have been the last people to leave Quarry Bank. I gather a disrespectful song was made up about my father setting out with the deeds to the house in one hand, and the canary in the other. The following day my father had his instructions to find his way back through the barricades in order to feed the chickens at our home!

We were allowed back about teatime the following day, so the evacuation hadn't lasted very long. No sooner were we back and the customers were coming round for their Christmas things. We all learned how Frank Webb had gone into the Liberal Club and shored-up the land mine. He later gave me a ring made from the metal casing of the land mine - and I've still got it today.

Soon after War broke out, I stopped working in Birmingham and went to Tube Fittings at Old Hill, then I went to Jones & Attwood in Stourbridge.

The parades and carnivals were the highlights of the year in Quarry Bank. Led by the town band, the decorated floats made their way to the park and everybody took part.

There were many Quarry Bank characters that I will always remember. One very important man was Dr. Maylett Smith. He used to come and visit my father on Sunday mornings and they would sit in the kitchen and have a pipe together. Dad used to give him a drink - which Mum complained used up our weekly profit!

I also remember Edwin. He taught everyone at the Sunday School to dance. He was a painter and decorator, from New Street, and worked for Sid Price. Edwin was very active in any charity fund-raising and was always involved in anything that was happening in Quarry Bank.

At Church there were the Dunns from Thorns Road, Mr. Hanke, and of course, Mrs. Warwick who was a "pillar of the church". Their manufacturing business was by the Blue Ball.

Left: Madge's mother, Ethel Maud Williams, stands on the right in this photograph. The lady wearing the cap is Polly Pritchard, who later became the Lady Mayor of Rowley Regis. (Madge Williams' Collection)

Ossie Biddle

The area where I was raised was Amblecote Road, between Quarry Bank and Brierley Hill. My Grandmother was tenant at The Black Horse Inn, Delph Road. The Black Horse was a second home to me. It was a family run pub: the family consisting of aunts and uncles - plus my parents - everyone doing their part in running the family business. They held the licence for more than seventy years.

I was born in January 1927, and I remember the early 1930s well. Times were very poor. Men and women were living on next to nothing and unemployment was part of everybody's lives. Homes were poorly lit and badly heated. Lighting was from paraffin lamps, candles, and some people had gas mantles. A fire was often made from coal stolen from local pit banks, or any logs that could be collected.

Home interiors were very basic with red quarry tiled floors, sometimes covered with podged rugs made out of old clothing material. Furniture was also very basic: a rough-scrubbed kitchen table, chairs, a chest of drawers which could be used on occasions as sleeping quarters for new-born babies. Large families were normal.

Cooking was done on an open fire, or on a range. These had ovens, and above the grate of a range there were often hooks on which to hang a kettle or pots. Water was usually heated in pots over open fires. Sleeping arrangements often involved three children sharing a bed, and boys and girls were often parted by a screen or a sheet dividing the room and providing some privacy. A toilet upstairs usually consisted of an enamel commode bucket or a chamber pot.

Washing was undertaken in the brew-house, in which there was a sink - generally brown in colour and made of earthenware, about four feet in length, plus two feet six inches wide and nine inches deep. The boiler built into the brew-house was used for everything - washing clothes, boiling puddings etc., and coal slack was burnt to heat the water. A galvanised tin bath was used for bathing, and Friday night was generally family bath night. After use the bath would usually be hooked on a nail fixed to the outside wall.

The lavatory was located down the back garden, and these would be emptied by workmen called night soilers. They worked in the early hours after midnight. A stand pipe water tap was shared in most cases, in what was known as "the yard".

Street lighting was provided from gas lamps - lit by a man called the lamp-lighter with the aid of a long rod or pole with a flame or pilot light attached. Children played games under these gas lamps at night such as marbles, jacks, skipping, Jack upon the mob stick etc. As it grew dark, mother or father would call the children in for bed - starting with the youngest.

Wedding parties were often held at The Black Horse, and you could expect these to be a rowdy day. The bride's and groom's families would often finish off the wedding day by falling out. Somebody would always state their son or daughter was no match for the other! It usually ended with a good shake of hands from both parties and the bride and groom would depart to the home of the in-laws - the end of a perfect day.

Community spirit was always strong. Help, if needed, was always available. A local lady was always at hand to act as midwife, not only assisting in bringing babies into the world, but also assisting at times of death. For times like these the Black Horse had a club, known as the Sick Death Club, which helped families at difficult times. A fee, of three pence a week, was paid into the club on each Saturday evening. Food was given to members, and it became quite a social evening.

I remember people turning their front room into mini-shops, selling bundles of wood, paraffin, candles, home-made toffee, pop, cooked meats etc.

But later in the 1930s employment improved. New housing schemes were being developed - Hawbush Road, the Thorns Estate etc., for example, and people were being moved from The Delph to new houses with bathrooms and inside toilets. As the prospect of War loomed, factories began to employ more labour - and when people started earning wages, they in turn spent more money in our pub.

Then war was declared on 3rd September 1939 and life became very difficult. Again rationing was introduced and fathers and sons were conscripted into the Armed Forces. Old people volunteered for service in the Home Guard, ARP, nursing etc. - everyone helping the community in good times and bad.

In the later part of the War eight American soldiers were billeted at our family pub, in readiness for the invasion of Europe. They became part of our family and very good friends to all those around us. They brought new life into our area and new hope of winning the War. I for one was very pleased to be associated with them. After months of being with us they left to take part of the invasion of Europe.

Gladys Davies

On 8th August 1941 I started work at the Delph Depot of the Dudley and Brierley Hill Gaslight Co., by which time the War had been on for two years.

Depots like the Delph were in all areas of the West Midlands, but they all worked independently, carrying out the job of making gas and coke, repairing gas leaks, fixing cookers, boilers, fires, and of course, the laying of service pipes - both inside and outside mains. A trained gas fitter did all these jobs, together with a fitter's boy, who was being trained. He would carry the fitter's tool bag for him, going everywhere on foot as there was no transport in those days. They became well known in their area, but after Nationalisation the provision of vans did away with all that.

During the War years coke was rationed to 1/4cwt per person. Every Saturday morning the queues would be from the Gas Office weighbridge to near the canal bridge in The Delph. They would come with prams, and wheelbarrows, in fact anything with wheels.

Street lighting was made possible by the lamp-lighter doing the rounds - lighting up in the evening, and turning off in the early morning. The start of the War had put paid to that as all streets were plunged into darkness - The Blackout. During this period, however, plans were made to convert all the lamps, so that when the lights came on again all over Britain, they would be automatic - no lamp-lighters, just lamp maintenance men. But even that was short-lived as gas lamps were replaced with electric lamps, first in the main roads and then in the side roads - and another era came to an end.

In 1949 the gas industry was nationalised, following in the footsteps of coal, electricity and transport. Apart from iron and steel, gas was the last to be nationalised by the post-War Labour Government - and we became the West Midlands Gas Board.

New offices were built at Bath Street, Dudley. Delph office staff, including me, were transferred to Dudley, and life was never the same. Today there is British Gas and lots of new names.

My working life ended on 11th February 1982 when I took early retirement after completing 40 years 7 months service. I thoroughly enjoyed my working life with the Gas Board, but was very glad that I was able to retire just as the computer age took over.

Pat Mattocks - Another Merry Hill

When I shop in Merry Hill, I cannot believe it is the same place where I grew up. I was born Pat Goodwin, and lived at "Bradwin" 75 Merry Hill. It was really quiet then; in fact we children used to roller skate round and round in big circles where there is now an island at the junction with Coppice Lane. Cars hardly ever used the road, Merry Hill to the Pedmore Road was just a track.

All the children in the street used to meet on the 'White Wall'. There must have been a house on the land at some stage before our time, but it was then just rough ground behind the wall, where we arranged the games we would play. Certain times of the year, out would come our tops and whips which we would colour with chalks or bits of coloured paper from a chocolate. We would spend ages on the patterns which changed when the top was spinning.

Then it would be skipping time. Everyone would bring out their ropes and do complicated moves. I remember one occasion when Coral Rubery had some childhood illness, measles or something, and couldn't mix with the other children. We devised a long skipping rope with Coral at one end and the rest of us at the other. Then it would be time for hop scotch. We drew the squares on the pavement and would polish up a piece of roof tile to slide into the numbered squares.

Of course, we did not have television then. Every week we would go to the Coronet Picture House which would become so full of children that some had to sit on boards on the floor at the front of the cinema. Mr. Roberts, the owner, would come round, followed by Arthur Hill. They shouted, "Quiet!" to keep us in order.

We also used to make camps on the banks, and fish for tadpoles in Warwick's pond. Our bonfires on 5th November were made from bats from the pit bonks, and they would still be alight days after Bonfire Night.

The winter of 1946/47 was very bad, but when the snow melted it flooded the tennis courts and we made a raft and floated around on a piece of fallen fence, using long sticks to steer ourselves. It was a great adventure.

Just past the Robin Hood Public House used to be where the gypsies spent the winter. Some of our neighbours were really frightened of the gypsies and used to hide under the stairs when they called at the door asking for water. The gypsies used to sell pegs and chrysanthemums which were carved from wood. They also told fortunes and sometimes said they would put a curse on you if you didn't cross their palm with silver. Sometimes us children would be asked by ladies from the Robin Hood Estate if we would walk them over the bonks as they were afraid of the gypsies.

We used to go to Cassin's Wood to pick bluebells in the Spring. We carried them back in arm fulls to put in jars on the kitchen window sills, but they always wilted before we got them home. What a waste!

When the weather was bad we used to paint or play board games, cards or knit or embroider. I remember when all the girls knit brown jumpers to wear at the Secondary School - but we couldn't wear them because we had knitted a bow in fairisle in our favourite colour on the front, and the uniform was strictly plain brown. We wore them after school to play in, but I wonder how many of today's ten-year-olds could knit themselves a jumper? Of course, they have other skills we knew nothing about - like computers and high-tech games - so they are just as clever really.

Merry Hill - road works in progress when this picture was taken in May 1958.

Frank Webb
The Night of the Land-mines.

The incident in which two land mines fell on Quarry Bank on Friday evening 19th December 1940 at 7.20pm., has become a local legend and because there was no loss of life the town earned the nick-name, "The Holy City". Various accounts of the event have been produced and these prompted Frank Webb to write his own account in 1989. Frank Webb was born in 1902 and he had first written some notes on this event in 1982.

Since my retirement at the age of eighty, I have been looking through old correspondence and have found several far from factual reports of the Quarry Bank Land-mines incident, and as I was the person most intimately concerned, considered it advisable that the actual facts be briefly recorded.

As Chairman of the Conservative club, I was conducting a meeting at the time of the incident. This was immediately cancelled and, as I was ARP Leader I assisted the Police in evacuating the area most likely to be affected, in case of the land-mines exploding.

At lunch time the following day, Saturday 20th December 1940, I received a telephone call from ARP Headquarters asking if I would meet a Naval Bomb Disposal Officer. We proceeded to the Liberal Club and found the land-mine in the first floor club room, covered with debris and standing in an almost vertical position, held only with parachute cords.

I was given directions as to which plates to remove to expose the time clock and two contact fuses, and was supplied with non-ferrous tools to carry out this operation, including a long cable. No shovel or other tools could be used because of the danger of creating an electrical field and consequent explosion. We then inspected the second land-mine which had crashed through the roof of some outbuildings on the opposite side of the road, and was lying in an almost horizontal position.

I then proceeded to the local Headquarters in Sun Street to collect volunteers and such planks and materials as would be necessary to lower the land-mines, which were approximately six foot high and two foot diameter, into a position where they could be defused. After the removal of the broken roof timbers and slates etc., the land-mine at the Liberal Club was detached from the parachute and lowered to the floor of the Club Room with the timing mechanism facing a window so that cable through the nearest window to open ground opposite the club.

I removed the plate and and exposed the time clock and fixed the claws attached to the cable to the wires at the rear of the time clock and we all pulled without success on two occasions because the claws slipped off the wires. For the third attempt I held the claws in position

and requested members of my party to try again. This time it was successful. As far as I can remember the time clock was approximately 8" in diameter. I then sent members of my party to a safe distance and removed the plate concealing two contact fuses which I removed and burnt in the roadway as instructed.

We then proceeded to the second land-mine and repeated the process and dragged the land-mine into the street for collection by the Bomb Disposal Squad who arrived the following morning. The Officer in charge of the Disposal Squad wanted to cut away part of the Liberal Club Room floor to enable the land-mine to be lowered to ground level. I objected to this and instead had a scaffold erected outside to enable the land-mine to be passed through the window and down a slide to a waiting vehicle. This avoided further damage to the Liberal Club premises. The second land-mine was easily loaded and the Bomb Disposal party left taking with them the parachutes.

The reward for our efforts was repaid by the return of the shop-keepers to their various premises to complete their weekend sales which had been so unexpectedly interrupted, and the safe return of members of the public to their respective homes. As Church Warden at the time, it was an inspiration to see the church full of local residents the following morning to show their relief and thankfulness for having avoided what could have been a tragedy with considerable loss of life.

The men who worked with Frank Webb were Charlie Williams, Harry Breeze, Fred Sidaway and Walter Bache. The latter died in a Japanese PoW camp in Burma, but the others survived the War and received a presentation to express the community's gratitude in 1949. In 1952 Mr. Ewart Bloore suggested that a sundial be erected in garden at the corner of Thorns Road and High Street to commemorate the event and the men's work, but this plan did not come to fruition.

The Liberal Club today.

Chapter 14
Quarry Bank Soldiers of the First World War

It seems that at least five hundred men left Quarry Bank to serve in the Armed Forces in the First World War. The Peace Memorial in Stevens Park lists 147 who gave their lives in doing so. **Patrick Shaw** has tried to identify these men and tell their story. Most Quarry Bank families lost a son, a father or a husband as a result of the war, and the names on the Memorial are all names found in Quarry Bank today, and in the pages of this book. Others survived and have contributed to the life of Quarry Bank since the conflict.

The research into Quarry Bankers who served in the Armed Forces during the First World War is ongoing. The notes and photographs reproduced here are simply the information that has been collected so far. Hopefully the comprehensive account can be published at later date.

The Quarry Bank Peace Memorial in Stevens Park was unveiled and dedicated on Saturday 24th October 1931. It was designed by Alfred Long, an architect of West Bromwich and was completed by several contractors. The bronze statue was the work of George Wade of London.

The Dedication began with an inter-denominational service at Christ Church, after which the choir led a procession of officials and ex-servicemen and relatives of the dead, down to the park. The "officials" were led by the Dean of Worcester and Ernest Stevens and consisted of all the Quarry Bank councillors plus representatives from surrounding towns. The Dean gave a long address, and there were further prayers and hymns. The event finished when two local buglers sounded the Last Post.

Above right   The memorial in Christ Church, Quarry Bank.

The Peace Memorial in Stevens Park. The seven bronze tablets list 147 "fallen" men from Quarry Bank. A second set of names of those who died in action in the Second World War was added on the right.

Three "Old Contemptibles"

The following three men were members of the Worcester Regiment who were killed in 1914:

Pte. Albert Perks
Died 1/11/14 of wounds sustained at the action at Gheluveldt near Ypres. He had been a reservist who was recalled in August 1914 to the 2nd Battalion from his employment with Mobberley & Perks of Thorns Road.

Pte. John James Greenaway
Was killed at Ypres while serving in C Company of the 3rd Battalion. He had enlisted at Dudley from his home at 13a Bower Lane.

Pte. Sidney John Pugh
Died of wounds sustained during the Battle of the Marne on 20/9/14 while serving with the 3rd Battalion. He had been in the Army for three years and had a brother, Alfred in the 1st Battalion. Their family home had been at 5 Stour Hill.

Dave Bennett, who supplied this information, adds that the 2nd and 3rd Battalions of the Worcesters both fought at Mons, were involved with the retreat and were decimated with the rest of the BEF at Ypres.

Ernest William Beddall
Joined as a private in the 1st Battalion of the Worcester Regiment and posted to France in 1915. He served in many battles, was promoted to Corporal and then Sergeant on 27/11/17. He was at the Battle of Bretonneux in April 1918. He and his brothers, Horace and Herbert, returned home safely.

Sergeant Ernest Beddall and Ada.   (Jack Beddall Clln.)

Pte. George Billingham
Joined the 3rd Battalion Worcester Regiment from his home at 21 Brick Kiln Street. He was killed in action in Flanders on 7/6/17. His medals are shown above.

Pte. Albert Blewitt
Died at the Battle of Festiburg on 17/5/15 while serving with the 2nd Battalion, Bedfordshire Regiment.

Lance Corp. Ernest Blewitt
Albert's brother. Killed in action at the Battle of the Somme on 1/7/16, serving with the 8th Battalion Kings Own Yorkshire Light Infantry. These men were step brothers to John Robinson of Mount Pleasant. (See page 84)

William Brookes
Joined C Battery of the Queens Artillery Regiment, which took him through the Hindenburg Line, and through Vimy Ridge at The Somme. He returned safely to Quarry Bank and worked until he was 79. He became Chairman of the local British Legion Branch, and he and his sons dug out the foundations for the new building in Park Road.

William Brookes, photographed 7/2/18.
(Mrs. A Reynolds Collection)

David William Capewell
Was born in Leek 7/3/1896, but moved to Quarry Bank as a boy. He joined the South Staffordshire Regiment in 1914, and was at the Battle of Ypres. Towards the end of the War he was taken prisoner but escaped. He made his own way back to the French Coast only to find the War had already ended.

When he returned to Quarry Bank he found work was short and therefore returned to the Forces - joining the RAF for three years. He later returned to Quarry Bank, where he lived until his death in July 1974.

David William Capewell's testimonial. (Joyce Webb)

2/Lieut T.H. Clee (Margaret Webb Collection)

2/Lieut. Thomas Howard Clee
Joined the Worcestershire Regiment and was killed on 7/11/18 at the age of 29. He is commemorated by the gift of a font to the Congregational Church in the high Street.

Frederick Cartwright
Frederick Cartwright was at a Territorial Army Camp in Minehead when war broke out - on his 22nd birthday. He was recalled to Kidderminster and joined the 7th Battalion of the Worcester Regiment, serving in Belgium and France. In 1917 he was sent back to England because his engineering skills were urgently required on munitions work - at Dudley. By 1918 he was urgently needed in France, where he joined the Machine Gun Corps. and served until the Armistice. He returned home and lived until 1977.

Frederick Cartwright. (Miss D.B. Cartwright Colln.)

Gunner Ernest Green
Born 26/10/1892, and lived at 34 Victoria Road. Joined the Royal Garrison Artillery, and killed in action on 18/7/17 at Ypres, at the age of 24, leaving a widow, Gertrude in Quarry Bank.

Right: Gunner E. Green.
(Gladys Davies Colln.)

103

Pte. Albert Edward Herrin
Albert Herrin, of Hill Street served with the 7th Battalion Leicestershire Regiment in France. He was taken prisoner and died, probably of starvation, as a PoW, 2/11/18

Right: Pte. Albert Herrin (Ethel Bloomer Collection)

Guardsman James Harold Herrin
James Herrin, Albert's cousin, from Sheffield Street served with the 2nd Grenadier Guards and died as a result of wounds on 29/9/17.

The Mason Brothers
Left: Able Seaman Howard Victor Mason, and right: his brother, Ernest Mason, in the Black Watch.

Pte. Harry O' Malley
Harry was born 23/11/1883 in High Street, Quarry Bank, and worked all his life as a chain-maker. He joined the South Staffordshire Regiment in September 1914 with his workmates - one of which was Daniel Plant. (See below) They fought in the Dardenelles, where Dan was killed. Just before the end of the War they were sent for by their employer who desperately needed their skills to complete war work. Although he came through the War without even a wound, he was disillusioned by the fact that he was laid off in peacetime whenever work was short. After a lifetime's work making chain he died in 1963.

James Harold Herrin (Ethel Bloomer Collection)

Harry O'Malley (Harry O'Malley Jnr.)

Daniel Plant (Bob Plant Collection))

The Marsh Brothers: Dan, John and Tom. (Mary Rousell)

Daniel Plant
Daniel Plant, Harry's workmate, was living in Delph Road when War broke out. They joined the South Staffordshire Regiment and went to France after some training. Daniel was killed in action on 29/9/16 by a shell burst on the Front Line. Daniel was 27 at the time, and his widow actually received the news of his death on her 27th birthday. His three year old son - also called Daniel - eventually managed to see his father's grave when he visited the Somme in 1966 on the 50th anniversary of the Battle.

Gunner Fred Rowley
Gunner Fred Rowley was killed in action in France on 17/9/17 at the age of 19.

Right: Gunner Rowley's parents donated this font to Cradley Forge church in his memory.

Above: John Norman Simmons   (June Groves' Collection)

Pte. Clifford Shaw
Clifford Shaw was a well known Sunday School teacher at Quarry Bank. He had married Lily Dunn, the Superintendents's daughter. He joined up in 1916 and was killed in action eleven months later, at the age of 28, while serving with the Northumberland Fusiliers.

Samuel Randle
Samuel was probably born in Deeley Street about 1897, and volunteered to join the Army when war broke out. He was taken prisoner, probably at the Battle of the Somme. He eventually returned to Quarry Bank and worked on the railway, but later re-joined the Army and went out east. He was interned by the Japanese in the Second World War, and there cannot be many men around here who were prisoners of the Germans in the First World War and prisoners of the Japanese in the Second. He survived all this and died after the War in Australia.

Cyril Vernon Sidaway
In "Quarry Bank in Old Photographs", we foolishly asserted that John Genner was the only Quarry Banker to don a kilt during the 1914-18 War. Ernest Mason and Cyril Sidaway also served with the Black Watch. Cyril served in Egypt and Turkey and the kilt was eventually made into a coat for his wife.
Below: Cyril V. Sidaway   (Doris Peat's Collection)

John Norman Simmons DCM.
Born in Brierley Hill, John Simmons lived all his life in Quarry Bank, taking an active part in the life of the community.

He led a distinguished military career in both World Wars. In the First World War he joined the 8th Battalion of the North Staffordshire Regiment when he was 19. By 1916 he was in the thick of war, and was awarded the Distinguished Conduct Medal on 6/6/18 at Bligny (Marne) when he took up the duties of Company Sergeant Major and reorganised the Company under heavy shell-fire.

On his return from the War, he worked 44 years at Round Oak Steel Works. He continued his military interests, rising to Major in the Army Cadet Force. For many years he was President of the Quarry Bank branch of the British Legion. He died in July 1987 in his 93rd. year.

Owen Stevens
Owen Stevens was an infantryman in the South Staffordshire Regiment. He fought in the Battle of the Somme and was gassed at Ypres. He survived the War, and eventually worked at Fort Dunlop in Birmingham, leaving Quarry Bank each morning at 5 o'clock to catch the train to Birmingham. He was a kind caring man who liked to play bowls in Stevens Park. He died in 1967 aged 72.

Left: Owen Stevens (Joyce Parkes Colln.)

Right: Albert Street from Queen Street also joined the Black Watch.
(Stan Street Collection)

Left: Jabez Batham
(Margaret Davies Colln.)

Jabez Batham

Ira Hampton recalls that his uncle, Jabez Batham was born in Quarry Bank in Hill Street in 1898, one of nine children. He worked as a sheet metal worker for Brettell & Shaw until enlisting in the 2/6th Battalion of the South Staffordshire Regiment in February 1917.

He was engaged in the Third Battle of Ypres, or Passchendaele, and the battalion suffered 20% losses while defending trenches near Zonnebeke. Jabez received stomach wounds and lay in a mud-filled trench for 24 hours until he was stretchered to a German Dressing Station, and thence via a Field Hospital to PoW Camp.

His parents were notified that he was 'missing - presumed dead', but early in 1918 the welcome news arrived that he was alive and was a PoW. He was discharged on 28th April 1919.

After the War, he set up a business hawking fruit and vegetables and fish around the streets of Quarry Bank with a horse and cart. He then opened a fruit and vegetable shop at 171 High Street. Behind the premises he bred and sold pigs. He also opened a newsagent and general store in Belmont Road, in the Lye. He died on 20th January 1964, aged 66.

Benjamin John Hill

Ben Hill, born 7/11/1894, lived in School Passage, Quarry Bank, and attended the Blue Coat School in Stourbridge from the age of seven. From 1909 onwards he worked at Noah Hingley's works in Netherton as a roll turner.

Ben enlisted on 31st August 1914 and joined the 8th Battalion of the South Staffordshire Regiment. He was killed by an overhead shell burst while repairing trenches on 29/2/1916 at the age of 21.

(Information supplied by Joy Richardson)

Herbert Stringer Yardley

Herbert Yardley was born in 1888 and lived in Ever Street as a young man. On 13th December he married Mabel Homer at Quarry Bank Church, and they had two sons and a daughter. Three months before the latter was born the family heard that he had been killed in Gallipoli on 6/8/1915, while serving with the 4th Battalion Worcester Regiment.

Below: Herbert Yardley's sacrifice was acknowledged by Quarry Bank UDC on this certificate, one of a number of such documents that still exist in Quarry Bank.
(Carol Bannister Collection)

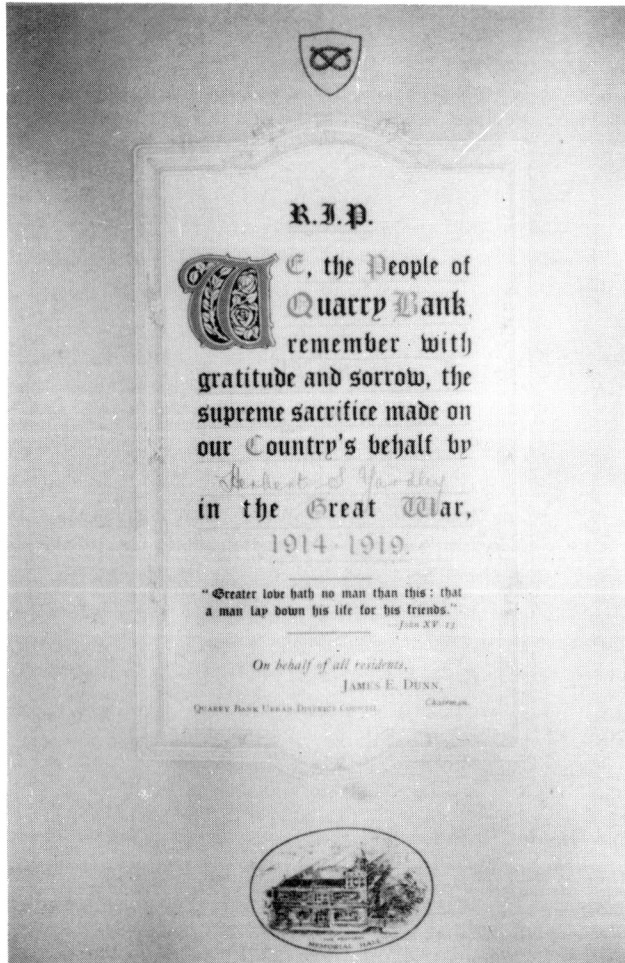

Ebenezer Round

Ebenezer was born in Quarry Bank on 1/5/1890. His family had a small holding near Mount Pleasant, but in the 1900s they emigrated to Australia. He joined the Australian Imperial Force, 11th Artillery Brigade and was killed in action in Belgium on 10/9/1917. It is believed that his brother Ezra was killed at Gallipoli.

Pte. Basil Tate

Basil Tate, of 21 Bower Lane, served in the 4th South Staffordshire Regiment, having enlisted on 25th November 1915. He earned the Military Medal during heavy fighting in April 1918. He was demobbed in March 1919 and returned to his job as a clerk on the Great Western Railway. His brother Frank also served, and was twice wounded.

(Paul Richardson's research for Mary Fletcher)

Right: Pte. Basil Tate wearing his Military Medal awarded for his actions on 10th April 1918 at the Battle of the Lys.

Far right: A silver cigarette case presented to Pte. Tate in April 1919 at the Conservative Club, when a "Roll of Honour" was unveiled and three soldiers were given these cases (Lieut. Frank Webb, Serg. A Whiley and Pte. Basil Tate)

Right: Isaac Robins (Stan Robins Colln.)

Isaac Robins
Isaac Robins, of 25 Victoria Road, was born about 1895. He served in Egypt and India with the Royal Flying Corps, later the RAF, as a mechanic. He survived the War and died in 1979.

Below: William Hanke

Above: Daniel Silcox, born 1899, of the 11th Battalion Leicestershire Regiment

William Hanke
William Hanke was stationed in Lancaster during the First World War, serving in the Royal Engineers. It was there that he met his wife Elizabeth Thompson, and they were married at Lancaster Parish Church in 1920.

They moved to Quarry Bank and lived in Birch Coppice. He started his engineering business in Talbots Lane. (See *"Quarry Bank in Old Photographs"* page 84.) He was keenly interested in the Church, and in politics. He was awarded the MBE for services to politics.

Pte. Arthur Saunders
Arthur came from 15 Level Woods, Mill Street and joined the 8th Battalion South Staffordshire Regiment. He died on 15/2/1916 at Ypres at the age of 19.

Pte. Joseph Bloomer
Joseph was born in Quarry Bank and enlisted with the 10th Battalion Worcestershire Regiment. He was killed in action on 3/7/1916.

Pte. John Edward Whitehouse
John Whitehouse came from 38 Ever Street, and enlisted at Stourbridge with the 1st/7th Battalion of the Worcestershire Regiment. He was killed in action on 18/7/1916.

William Jones
William Jones was born in Quarry Bank and enlisted in Brierley Hill, apparently joining the Durham Light Infantry. He later transferred to the 2nd/5th Battalion of the Manchester Regiment and was killed in action on 5/10/1917.

Pte. Wilf Johnson
Wilf joined the 3rd Battalion, Worcestershire Regiment and was killed in action on 27/7/1915. Ironically his widow received the news just after the death of their only child.

Pte Arthur Taylor
Arthur Taylor of the 2nd Worcestershire Regiment became well known locally as a result of a visit to Quarry Bank while convalescing from treatment to a bullet wound. Messrs Brettell & Shaw, his previous employer, paid for the visit to his wife and child, living in West Street on 23 August 1915. At the time it was still thought that such events encouraged support for the War, rather than exposed its horrors. Arthur was killed later during the War.

Pte. Joseph Attwood
Joseph Attwood joined the 1st/5th Battalion of the South Staffordshire Regiment and took part in the charge against the Hohenzollern Redoubt of 1915, in which he was killed.

Pte William Round
Serving with the 8th Battalion South Staffords, Stretcher-bearer William Round of Quarry Bank was killed on 10/7/1917.

Below: Left to right: The 1914-15 Star, the War Medal, and the Victory Medal, (front and back).

Gunner David Homer
David Homer of Victoria Road enlisted in 1916 and was killed in France a year later on 16/6/1917, but he does not seem to have qualified to be included on the Peace Memorial.

Pte Albert Bennett
Albert served with the 8th Battalion West Riding Regiment and was wounded on 9th August 1917 and died ten days later.

Pte James Billingham
James, of New Street, served with the 1st Battalion Monmouthshire Regiment and was killed on 25/8/17 at the age of 33.

Pte. Aquilla Dunn
Aquilla Dunn of New Street joined the 8th Battalion Northumberland Fusiliers, was killed on 29/10/1917.

Pte George Cox
George Cox of 32 Ever Street left Bennett's the chain manufacturers to join up at the outbreak of the War. He joined the Royal Army Ordnance Corps. and died on 8th Dec. 1917 in a hospital in France, leaving a widow and three children.

Pte. Samuel Clarke
Sam Clarke of 16 Sheffield Street served with the Lancashire Fusiliers, and died towards the end of 1917 after being badly wounded.

Lieut. Frank Dutton
Frank was the son of Mrs. Dutton, High Street, Quarry Bank, and step brother to J. Foxall, the hairdresser in the High Street. Was a reservist who went to France with the RFA when war broke out. Twice wounded and twice gassed, he was rapidly promoted. He was expecting further promotion when he was posted as "missing" in March 1918. At the age of 28 he left a widow and two children.

Pte. John Thomas Hickman
John joined up in April 1917. Killed 29/6/1918, aged 21.

Sergeant Horace Dodson
Joined the RAF and died of pneumonia in France on 9/11/1918 soon afterwards. His parents kept The gate Hangs Well in Bower Lane.